A Walk
with
Four Spiritual
Guides

Related books:
SkyLight Illuminations Series

Bhagavad Gita: Annotated & Explained

Dhammapada: Annotated & Explained

The Gospel of Thomas: Annotated & Explained

Selections from the Gospel of Sri Ramakrishna: Annotated & Explained

The Way of a Pilgrim: Annotated & Explained

Zohar: Annotated & Explained

Andrew Harvey, series editor

A Walk
with
Four Spiritual Guides

Krishna, Buddha,
Jesus, and Ramakrishna

ANDREW
HARVEY

Walking Together, Finding the Way
SKYLIGHT PATHS Publishing
Woodstock, Vermont

A Walk with Four Spiritual Guides:
Krishna, Buddha, Jesus, and Ramakrishna

Foreword and introductions © 2003 by Andrew Harvey

Selections from:
Bhagavad Gita: Annotated & Explained © 2001 by Kendra Crossen Burroughs;
translation by Shri Purohit Swami
Dhammapada: Annotated & Explained © 2002 by SkyLight Paths Publishing;
translation by Max Müller, annotations by Jack Maguire
The Gospel of Thomas: Annotated & Explained © 2002 by Stevan Davies
Selections from the Gospel of Sri Ramakrishna: Annotated & Explained © 2002 by Kendra
Crossen Burroughs; translation by Swami Nikhilananda

Library of Congress Cataloging-in-Publication Data
Harvey, Andrew, 1952–
A walk with four spiritual guides : Krishna, Buddha, Jesus, and
Ramakrishna / Andrew Harvey.
      p. cm.
ISBN 1-893361-73-X (hardcover)
1. Spiritual life. 2. Religions. I. Title.
BL624.H3445 2003
291.4—dc21
2002154848

10 9 8 7 6 5 4 3 2 1
Manufactured in Canada

SkyLight Paths Publishing is creating a place where people of different spiritual traditions come together for challenge and inspiration, a place where we can help each other understand the
mystery that lies at the heart of our existence.

SkyLight Paths sees both believers and seekers as a community
that increasingly transcends traditional boundaries of religion and
denomination—people wanting to learn from each other, *walking
together, finding the way.*

SkyLight Paths, "Walking Together, Finding the Way" and colophon are
trademarks of LongHill Partners, Inc., registered in the U.S. Patent and
Trademark Office.

Walking Together, Finding the Way
Published by SkyLight Paths Publishing
A Division of LongHill Partners, Inc.
Sunset Farm Offices, Route 4, P.O. Box 237
Woodstock, VT 05091
Tel: (802) 457-4000   Fax: (802) 457-4004
www.skylightpaths.com

To Leila and Henry Luce III
for all the joy of their long love

Contents ☐

Foreword ☐

It is early December 1992. I am sitting with the eighty-six-year-old Catholic monk and mystic Father Bede Griffiths in his hut in the South Indian morning waiting for an Australian crew, who is making a film of his life, to arrive. I am the host of the documentary. For eight marvelous days, Bede and I have been talking about God, the Church, the World's mystical traditions, and the various stages of that search for truth that brought him to India forty years before.

Bede paused suddenly (we had been talking about his early love of the romantic poets) and then said, quietly and intensely, "You know, of course, Andrew, that we are now in the hour of God."

Although it was a warm, fragrant morning, I shivered.

"When you say 'hour of God,' what do you mean?"

"I mean that the whole human race has now come to the moment when everything is at stake, when a vast shift of consciousness will have to take place on a massive scale in all societies and religions for the world to survive. Unless human life becomes centered on the awareness of a transcendent reality that embraces all humanity and the whole universe and at the same time transcends our present level of life and consciousness, there is little hope for us."

His calm, measured, aristocratic voice made his words all the more arresting. Bede coughed and gazed at his fine, strong, bony hands.

"Very few people dare to face how extreme and decisive the situation has now become. The churches and religions are fossilized in their old dogmas and divisions. What I see of the 'New Age' on my travels in America fills me with some hope, but I am aware of the naivete and escapism of a great deal of what passes for spirituality in it. Very few people are prepared to look without illusion at our time and see it for what it is—a crucifixion on a worldwide scale of everything humanity has expected or trusted or believed in every level and in every arena. To look like this requires a kind of final faith and courage, which few have as yet. You and others like you will have to live and write in such a way as to help people to such a faith and trust."

I had never, in all the many hours we had spent together, heard him speak so nakedly and darkly about the future of the world, and I knew him well enough already to know that he never said anything without deep purpose.

We sat together in silence, absorbing the pain and challenge of his words. Then I asked, "Do you think humanity can get through?"

"Of course," he said immediately, his voice strong, "but it will cost everything. Just as Jesus had to go through death into the new world of the Resurrection, so millions of us will have to go through a death to the past and to all old ways of being and doing if we are going to be brought by the grace of God into the truth of a real new age. The next twenty years will unfold a series of terrible disasters, wars, and ordeals of every kind that will reveal if the human race is ready to die into new life or not. I have no idea of what the outcome of the savage period we are entering will be. There are many prophecies in many mystical traditions that speak of the horror of this time, but they disagree as to what will happen. This I think shows that either total destruction or total transformation is possible and depend on us, on what we choose, and how we act."

Bede paused again, turning his head to look at me directly. "I know for certain only two things about the time we are about to enter. The first is that it will see on every level a ruthless battle between those forces that want to keep humanity enslaved to the past—and these include religious fundamentalism, nationalism, materialism, and corporate greed—and those forces that will awaken in response to a hunger for a new way of living and of doing everything. The second thing I know—and I know this from my own inmost experience—is that God will shower help, grace, and protection on all those who sincerely want to change and are brave enough to risk the great adventure of transformation."

Very softly, Bede added, "God, I believe, wants a new world and a new humanity to be born from what is about to unfold. Whether we really do or not and whether we are prepared to pay the price and accept the responsibility for changing, I do not know. You, my dear Andrew, and your generation will find out. Wherever I am, I will be with you, and praying for your courage and strength."

That was in 1992. The world is now plunged in that "hour of God" of which Bede spoke so starkly. The "disasters, wars, and ordeals" that he foretold from the calm of his Indian hut rage around us. Fundamentalism is on the rise everywhere and terrorism has increased to an unprecedented level, creating international instability that could have incalculably horrific consequences. And the squalid failure of recent international summits have revealed, yet again, how little resolve the so-called civilized world can muster to deal with the now potentially terminal state of the environment.

From all sides, the news is bad, very bad. World population now stands at 6.1 billion (already 2 billion more than experts of sustainable growth recommend). By 2050, it could expand as much as 50 percent, to 9.3 billion, overwhelming even the best-intentioned international plans to adjust poverty levels and share resources. In a world in which parts of the West live in a high-tech luxury unimaginable even when I was speaking with Bede in 1992, a staggering 2.8 billion people live in conditions of squalor and disease and deprivation of every kind on less than two dollars a day. Air, sea, and land resources are being used 20 percent faster than they can be replenished—and this according to the conservative estimates of the World Wildlife Fund. The Arctic and Antarctic ice caps are melting and, according to many experts, global warming is proceeding even faster than the most depressed doomsayers of the 1980s and 1990s forecasted. About 1.1 billion people lack access to safe drinking water, mainly in Africa and Asia.

It has never been clearer that the "vast shift of consciousness on a massive scale" that Bede Griffiths called for is humanity's last hope. Without such a shift and a radical new openness to divine wisdom and guidance, all the solutions we propose to deal with our increasingly overwhelming problems will be crippled by the very assumptions that created the problems in the first place. The human race has been brought by its own inner destiny and by God to a place where it must leap into a new kind of being or be destroyed by the folly of its own greed and ignorance. Anyone who sees this clearly has no option but to do everything in his or her power to transform themselves enough to be really and radically useful, to go through the "death" to the past that Bede spoke of and be reborn in the new consciousness that the Divine is trying to birth everywhere, whatever the price.

I have found in my own struggle to change and be changed that my chief sources of inspiration have sprung from the mystical traditions of the past. In their great scriptures and practical technologies of transformation, I have found at once a noble vision of human-divine identity and the means to realize and embody its truth and power in reality. From them, I have drunk the wines of fearlessness and ecstasy and slowly learned how, again and again, to risk everything and to welcome the deaths that transfigure and empower. They have taught me rigor and illusionless hope and the courage to endure in joy.

Here, in this little book, you will meet four of humanity's greatest guides: Krishna, Buddha, Jesus, and Ramakrishna. From each of them you will learn priceless and practical lessons that will inspire you to become a warrior of love and knowledge and a servant of that one transformed future that could enable us to survive.

From Krishna's sublime teachings in the Bhagavad Gita, you will learn how to become a selfless instrument of the Divine in reality and how to act in harmony with the Divine Will while giving up all fruits of action. From the Buddha you will learn how to train your mind and heart in that equanimity and compassion that in a terrible time create timeless inner oases of peace and strength. From the Jesus of the Gospel of Thomas, you will learn of a mystical fire that burns down the house of the past and how to become one with that fire and be one of its revolutionary agents in the real. From Ramakrishna, you will learn of the mercy, splendor, and grandeur of the Motherhood of God and of the spiritual sincerity and ardor you need to have to be in touch with it and strengthened by its power.

Combining and fusing all the wisdom of the voices of these great lovers of God within the context of humble, daily spiritual practice and a commitment to put the principles of love and justice into action in the world, you will slowly but marvelously discover sources of passion, delight, and endurance within you that you could never have suspected. You will discover capacities for heroic love and sacrifice you would have never imagined. These will illumine your life with meaning, whatever happens around you or to you. These will make you brave and keep you inspired, however sickening the times become.

At the end of my conversation with Bede Griffiths that morning, in 1992, I asked him, "Do you sometimes wish you had been born in easier times?"

He gazed at me in genuine astonishment and then a beautiful smile lit up his face. "Good heavens, no!" he said. "An age like this compels you to be serious about God and change. One thing I have learned again and again is that whatever God brings you to, God will bring you through—if you love, surrender, give, risk, and open yourself enough."

May the teachings in this book help us all to "love, surrender, give, risk, and open enough," and in time!

1 ▪ Krishna

Krishna and Arjuna

Walking with Krishna ☐

When I was twenty-five I left England and the plush but sterile academic life I was leading there to wander for a year around India. During that year I found myself living in Pondicherry at the ashram of Sri Aurobindo, where, with awe and amazement, I read the Bhagavad Gita for the first time, and where I was lucky enough to find in an old ashramite, whom I shall call "Mr. Bannerjee," the ideal first guide to its mysteries. Every morning at dawn for a month Mr. Bannerjee, immaculate, wizened, screechy-voiced, clothed in blazing white, and seated in the lotus position, took me through the Gita in the Sanskrit, translating as he went, with baroque exuberance.

On our first meeting he gazed solemnly at me and said, "There are four things you must not forget when it comes to understanding the Gita. The first is that, although it is considered the spiritual masterpiece of Hinduism, its message is timeless and universal and transcends all religion. Note here too, by the way, that 'Hinduism' is itself a name imposed on a whole slew of different cults and faiths by the Greeks who followed Alexander the Great into India. The essence of all of these philosophies— and of religious life itself—is found in the Gita.

"The second thing you must remember if you are ever to pierce the mystery of this spiritual masterpiece is this: The dialogue it enshrines between the divine avatar Krishna and the soldier Arjuna on the battlefield of Kurukshetra is always taking place within the heart and soul of every human being on the battlefield of this terrible and beautiful world. Each one of us contains the doubting, despairing, potentially brave and illumined human being (Arjuna) and the mystery of Krishna (the eternal Divine Self) hidden behind all the veils of our psyche and mind. What the Gita does is dramatize in the most inspired way imaginable and for all time the full truth of this dialogue and the initiation it can make possible into full human divine life.

"The third thing that will help you approach the Gita's mystery with wisdom is to know that you cannot read it as a 'text' or even as a great and sublime mystical poem only. You must approach it slowly, reverently, bringing to your reading of it the whole range of your inner and outer experience and all of the pressing, disturbing questions of your life and search. Only then will the Gita be able to enter your blood and work its holy magic in the core of your being.

"The fourth and last thing that will open to you the doors of the Gita's splendor is to forget all the academic and religious arguments about which of the different 'yogas' or 'ways of divine union' it celebrates. Different schools bias the interpretation of the text to their own vision. The full truth is that the Gita embodies and celebrates a permanently radical fusion of all the traditional Hindu approaches to the Divine in a vision of what the full human divine being should and must be. These different yogas are in the Gita fused into a vision that combines and transcends them all to offer human beings the richest and most complete way of being and acting in the world with divine truth, wisdom, and effectiveness."

In our last class, which took place four marvelous, wild weeks later, Mr. Bannerjee added a fifth prerequisite for reading the Gita: "Always read the Bhagavad Gita as if it had just been written and as if it were referring to what is going on in the world right now. If you do, you will find that its power to initiate and inspire is constantly astounding. The Gita was probably written more than two thousand years ago; each different cycle of world civilization will find in it new truth, expressed with permanently fresh urgency."

Now that I have been graced with the chance to introduce others to this masterpiece, I must take up Mr. Bannerjee's challenge and try to express as succinctly as I can what the Gita is saying to me and other seekers, now, at the beginning of the twenty-first century. Its message, I believe, could not be more urgent, or more relevant to the deepest problems and challenges facing humanity.

I believe that the whole of humanity is now in the thick of a battle whose outcome will determine the fate of the planet. This battle is between those forces of life that want to see us living in harmony with the creation, inspired by divine love, and so able to re-create our devastated world with the powers of the Divine itself, and the forces of death—of ignorance, pride, and greed—that have brought us to the moment where we have almost destroyed nature and polluted the world's mind and heart with violence and a materialistic vision of humanity so reductive that it threatens us all with despair and meaninglessness at a moment when hope and resolve are crucial. This tremendous battle is being fought out in every arena of our life—in politics, industry, the arts, the sciences, the universities, the media, and in the depths of all of our psyches.

The signs are not encouraging. We have known about the progressive degradation of the environment for more than twenty years now, but almost nothing significant has been done to counteract it. Two billion people are now living in poverty, yet our addiction to an economic system that thrives on such desolation continues unabated. Much of organized religion continues to be largely divisive, drunk on outmoded visions of exclusive truth, and wedded to a vision of the Divine that obsessively adores transcendence at this moment when the entire immanent body of God-Nature is in mortal danger. The majority of modern seekers in the so-called New Age who pride themselves on participating in a mystical renaissance are in fact largely trapped in a narcissistic coma, apolitical, unconcerned by and blind to the approaching potentially terminal tragedy of the destruction of nature.

Despair, however, is a luxury those who are growing awake in this darkness cannot afford; all those who see the extent of the potential danger and tragedy threatening humanity and nature are compelled to respond with the deepest of themselves. In the Bhagavad Gita, those who long to know how to fight wisely for the future will find a handbook of spiritual warriorhood and divine realization that will constantly inspire and ennoble them and infuse them with divine truth and sacred passion.

It is clear, I think, to anyone who sees the depth of the global predicament we are in that there can only be one way out now—the way out of "mystical activism." An activism that is not fed by mystical wisdom and stamina will wither in the fire of persistent and persistently exhausting disappointment and defeat and tend to create as many new problems as those it tries to solve. A mysticism that is not committed to action within the world on behalf of the poor, of the oppressed, and of nature itself condemns itself to futility at a moment when so much is at stake. Only the highest spiritual wisdom and tireless sacred passion for all of life united with pragmatic, radical action on all possible fronts can now help us preserve the planet. The Gita can guide us to this all-transforming fusion of vision and action because, with the Gospels, it is the most wise and challenging celebration of it.

This, then, in plain language, is what I believe is our "inner Krishna's" message to each of us now, as expressed in the Gita: First of all, like Arjuna, face the truth of the battle that rages on all sides in the world; do not indulge in despair, and claim your own spiritual warriorhood.

Second, realize as quickly and as completely as possible your divine identity and origin through whatever way of divine union your temperament opens up to you—whether it is of knowledge or of devotion. Only such an experience of the Divine in and as you will give you the calm, fearlessness, strength, and detachment you will need to be focused, effective, and undeterred.

Third, understand fully and finally the necessity of surrendering your will and the fruit of your actions wholly to the Divine. There are two reasons why this is essential. Total surrender of your will and actions will enable the Divine to use both for its own transforming purposes without the interference of your false self and its mind-concocted agendas. It will also give you direct access to the Divine's own timeless resources of inner peace and inexhaustible sacred passion, which will enable you to stay true to your purpose and your mission whatever defeats or disappointments happen along the way. Through this surrender to God of your will and of the fruits of your actions, become a poised instrument of the Divine's own sacred plan for humanity, and whatever you do will be the Divine acting in you and through you—and so far more useful and transformative than any other form of action, however well intentioned or "inspired."

Fourth, when you have really absorbed the lessons of this wisdom of surrender, understand with your whole being that it is not in the end austere or harsh. In fact, it will open to you, as the last wonderful pages of the Gita reveal, a final mystery of divine love that will fill your whole being with a permanent sober ecstasy—an ecstasy that arises from the awareness that you and all beings are loved by God with deathless and unconditional love. And this ecstasy will unveil to you and in you the fullness of your divine humanity.

If you fuse knowledge of your transcendent origin with tireless service in and for God in the ways the Gita makes plain to you, you will come, on earth and in this body, to know divine joy and be fed by the ceaseless passion-energy of divine love. Human and divine, inner peace and outer action, knowledge and love, will be married in you at ever-greater depths to make you an ever more powerful and radiant warrior for Love and Justice in all dimensions.

The message of the Gita is one of perfect spiritual balance. It challenges fundamentally both those materialistic visions that think of humanity and the universe in purely scientific or practical terms and those religious visions of the Divine that see the world as imperfect or merely an illusion. If we listen to this message both in its complexity and in its urgency, we will come to the wonder, bliss, and empowerment of Arjuna himself at the end of this "Song of God." And with more and more of us empowered in this calm and glorious way, the future of our world will, at last, be in wise hands.

Krishna and his devotee Radha represent divine love.

Krishna and the Bhagavad Gita ☐

Kendra Crossen Burroughs

The best-loved of all Indian scriptures is the Bhagavad Gita—often called simply the Gita ("song"). In English its title might be rendered as "Song of the Blessed One" or "Song of the Adorable One." The Adorable One is Lord Krishna, who is God in human form, and the Song is his teaching to humanity.

What the Gita Is About

The teaching of the Gita emerges from a battlefield conversation between Lord Krishna and the warrior-prince Arjuna. The war—which is said to have taken place in India about five thousand years ago—is between two royal families, the Kauravas ("descendants of Kuru") and the Pandavas ("sons of Pandu"). The long story of how this conflict came about is told in the Mahabharata, India's vast national epic, of which the Bhagavad Gita is the sixth chapter.

The Kauravas are the "bad guys," who deprived their cousins the Pandavas of their rightful kingdom. The Pandavas enter the fight only after their efforts at compromise have failed. Even Krishna—a cousin of the Pandava princes—could not make peace with the evil Kauravas. Krishna would not fight, but he offered Duryodhana, chief of the Kaurava army, a choice between his presence and his army. Duryodhana chose the army, so Krishna granted his presence to the Pandavas by serving as Arjuna's charioteer.

The narrative opens with the blind king Dhritarashtra (father of one hundred sons, the Kauravas), in his palace, asking his minister Sanjaya to tell him about the battle. Through supernatural perception (granted by

Vyasa, the author of the Mahabharata, who also appears in the epic as a grandfather of the Pandavas), Sanjaya describes the scene taking place on the distant battlefield. As fighting is about to begin, Arjuna asks Krishna to draw up their chariot between the two armies so that he may survey them. As he views his opponents, Arjuna is suddenly overcome with despair at the prospect of killing his own relatives, friends, and mentors. Realizing the terrible consequences of war, the great archer casts down his bow and arrow, unwilling to fight. The rest of the Gita is Krishna's teaching in response to Arjuna's anguish.

After the Bhagavad Gita is concluded, the Mahabharata goes on to tell how Krishna leads the Pandavas to victory in a battle between divine and demonic forces that lasts for eighteen days. Krishna as the divine incarnation, or Avatar, has succeeded in rekindling the torch of Love and Truth on the eve of a new world-age—the degenerate period known as the *kali yuga* in which we find ourselves today.

Who Wrote the Gita?

According to Hindu tradition, the author of the Mahabharata (including the Gita) was the sage Vyasa, whose name means "compiler." He is said to have also compiled the Vedas, ancient texts based on revelations received by various seers *(rishis)* while in a superconscious state. Thus, although the Gita is officially classed among the texts known as "traditions" (*smriti*, "remembered" knowledge), it has attained the status of a divine revelation (*shruti*, "heard" knowledge that is eternally existent), similar to the Vedas. The Gita is sometimes also called an Upanishad, the term used for mystical writings that convey the "hidden meaning" of the Vedas concerning the true goal of life and how to attain it. If the Upanishads are the cream of the milk of the Vedas, then the Gita is said to be the butter churned from the cream. The philosophy based on the Upanishads is known as Vedanta, and the Bhagavad Gita has been deemed "the best authority on Vedanta."

Contemporary secular scholars consider Vyasa to be a legendary figure and not the literal author of the Gita. They date the composition of the

Mahabharata to sometime between the fifth and second centuries B.C.E. and believe that the Gita was added to the epic at a later time. To account for apparent discrepancies in the text, such scholars attribute the Mahabharata to several different authors. In terms of chronology, one ordinary human being could not have literally written both the Vedas and the Mahabharata. Tradition nonetheless regards Vyasa as a single individual, although not an ordinary human being. According to some authorities, the name of a *rishi* designates not only a specific individual but also a characteristic state of consciousness, along with its functions, which is shared by different historical figures who may bear the same name in the literature. Regarded in this light, the attribution of the Bhagavad Gita to Vyasa is more understandable.

The Language of the Gita

The Bhagavad Gita has been translated into all the major languages of the world—as well as some minor ones, including Yiddish. The original text was written in Sanskrit, the ancient language of India in which the Hindu scriptures and a vast body of poetry and literature were composed. Technically a "dead" language, Sanskrit is currently spoken only by Vedic scholars, known as pandits, and a small group of revivalists. It is, however, the ancestor of modern Indian languages and an older relative of most modern Western languages as well.

Sanskrit is regarded as a sacred language, and its sound is held to have a powerful transforming effect. The Gita is usually recited as a chant, and listening to a recitation of it in Sanskrit is considered uplifting even if one doesn't understand the words.

An unrhymed poem, the Gita is mostly in what is called the *shloka* meter, consisting of four lines of eight syllables each—the translator Winthrop Sargeant compares it to the meter of Longfellow's *Hiawatha* ("By the shores of Gitchee Gumee"...). A number of stanzas are in the *tristubh* meter, consisting of four lines of eleven syllables each, used during dramatic moments.

Interpreting the Gita

Numerous pandits and gurus as well as Western scholars have written commentaries on the Gita. The various interpretations do not always agree, and there are many points of controversy. Does the Gita teach monism, monotheism, or dualism? Does it favor the dualistic Samkhya philosophy or the nondualistic Vedanta? The path of knowledge or the path of devotion? Action or inaction? Theism, pantheism, or panentheism? The teaching that the world is real or illusory? Arguments have been made for all of these competing perspectives. A traditional view holds that they are not disagreeing but rather looking at different facets of the same gem. As the Vedas state, truth is ever the same, though the wise speak of it in various ways.

Despite the controversies, most readers can agree that the heart of the Gita's message is "Love God." Perhaps the Gita is best read intuitively rather than analytically. The great modern sage Sri Aurobindo advises us not to be overly concerned with how the Gita was understood in its own place and time; rather we should extract from it the living truths that meet our own spiritual needs, for the Gita's spirit is large, profound, universal, and timeless. As stated in the *Encyclopedia of Religion,* the text "changes with each reader, fluctuates in meaning with each successive generation of interpreters, which is to say, it lives. This vitality constitutes its sacrality."

Krishna as God in Human Form

An important feature of the Gita's teaching is Krishna's identity as the Avatar (from Sanskrit *avatara,* "descent"). The Avatar, who is God directly "descended" into human form (as contrasted with a human being who "ascends" to a state of God-consciousness), appears on earth periodically—in different forms, under different names, in different parts of the world—to restore truth in the world and to shower grace on the lovers of God. In the Vedic tradition, Krishna is worshiped as an Avatar of Vishnu, that aspect of the one indivisible God which preserves and protects the creation. Yet many people regard him as a universal savior comparable to (or even identical with) such world teachers as Christ and Buddha.

The Gita makes clear that Krishna is the Supreme Deity and not simply "a god." This does not mean, however, that only the advent of God as Krishna is worthy of worship, or that any one divine incarnation is superior to any other: all God-realized beings are one in consciousness, because God is always one and the same. As Aurobindo writes, the Avatar, "though he is manifest in the name and form of Krishna, lays no exclusiveness on this one form of his human birth, but on that which it represents, the Divine, the Purushottama [Supreme Spirit], of whom all Avatars are the human births."

Although the name Krishna is usually translated as "Black" or "Dark Blue," some translators give the meaning as "Puller," because Krishna draws the hearts of all beings to himself. Stories about Krishna in the collections of legends known as the Puranas celebrate his irresistibly loving and lovable nature—as a mischievous child and youth, playing his enchanting flute and attracting the devotion of the cowherding girls and boys (for Krishna himself was chief of the cowherds). Swami Nikhilananda writes: "No eyes ever had enough of the exquisite beauty of Krishna, the dark-blue form clad in a yellow robe, a garland of wild flowers hanging from His neck, and a peacock feather adorning His crest." This playful and adorable aspect of Krishna is less obvious in the Gita, where attention is drawn more to his role as wise teacher and compassionate friend.

Many writers treat Krishna as a figure of mythology and question whether such a historical personage ever existed; or else they say he was a human hero who was later divinized. A similar controversy is taking place about the historical Jesus versus the mythic Christ. In both cases—and especially in Krishna's, since his advent was so long ago—it is not possible to establish the facts in terms of contemporary methodology. History and legend are now bound too closely to untangle. On the other hand, just as Christian tradition holds that the Gospel accounts were inspired by the Holy Spirit and are not merely the product of their human authors, so too, according to the Vedic tradition, the testimonials of the seers regarding Krishna's advent are based on mystical knowledge that is not merely a fanciful exaggeration of facts but rather a deeper insight into reality arising from advanced states of consciousness.

Aurobindo comments that to the spiritual aspirant, controversies over historicity are a waste of time: the Krishna who matters to us is the eternal incarnation of the Divine that we know by inner experience, not the historical teacher and leader. For his lovers, Lord Krishna is a living reality whose companionship is possible to experience here and now, as devotees of all times (including our own) will attest. The Divine Beloved is always with us and within us, because God *is* our own Self. The Avatar is like the sun, which never actually disappears, even though from our limited perspective it appears to vanish at sunset. This divine presence can be felt when one reads the Gita with a spirit of devotion.

For many people in the world, not only Hindus, reading or reciting a portion of the Bhagavad Gita is part of their daily spiritual practice. The hearts of many others have been touched by reading it only once with openness to the transforming power of the words of Lord Krishna. May you be so blessed.

Selections from the Bhagavad Gita

1 "Aryan" derives from the Sanskrit *arya* ("noble" or "honorable"), a word applied in ancient times to great spiritual personalities. Western scholars adopted the term to designate a category of Indo-Iranian languages as well as an ethnic or racial group, also known as "Indo-Europeans." These Aryans were a fair-skinned nomadic people believed to have migrated in prehistoric times from the plains north of the Caucasus, some tribes settling in northern Europe, others in Iran and northern India. The "Aryan invasion" of India has been questioned by authors such as Georg Feuerstein and David Frawley, who argue that the Sanskrit-speaking Vedic Aryans were not foreign invaders but indigenous inhabitants of India. The Nazis promoted the fiction, concocted in Europe in the nineteenth century, of a morally superior "Aryan race," of which Nordic or Germanic peoples were supposedly the purest examples.

2 Effeminacy: The Sanskrit original means "weakness of heart." "In this world which baffles our reason, violence there will always be. The Gita shows the way which will lead us out of it, but it also says that we cannot escape it by running away from it like cowards" (Gandhi).

3 As it happened, so many arrows were shot into Bhishma during the battle that he was able to lie parallel to the ground, supported by the arrow shafts. This event furnished the model for the well-known "bed of nails" used by some Indian ascetics. Bhishma lay on his bed of arrows and waited to die until the sun turned north, thus choosing an auspicious moment for his death.

☐ The Philosophy of Discrimination: Samkhya Yoga

1 Sanjaya then told how the Lord Shri Krishna, seeing Arjuna over-whelmed with compassion, his eyes dimmed with flowing tears and full of despondency, consoled him.

The Lord said:

2 My beloved friend! Why yield, just on the eve of battle, to this weakness which does no credit to those who call themselves Aryans,**1** and only brings them infamy and bars against them the gates of heaven?

3 O Arjuna! Why give way to unmanliness? O you who are the terror of your enemies! Shake off such shameful effeminacy,**2** make ready to act!

Arjuna argued:

4 My Lord! How can I, when the battle rages, send an arrow through Bhishma**3** and Drona, who should receive my reverence?

5 Rather would I content myself with a beggar's crust than kill these teach-ers of mine, these precious noble souls! To slay these masters who are my benefactors would be to stain the sweetness of life's pleasure with their blood.

6 Nor can I say whether it were better that they conquer me or for me to conquer them, since I would no longer care to live if I killed these sons of Dhritarashtra, now preparing for fight.

7 My heart is oppressed with pity, and my mind confused as to what my duty is. Therefore, my Lord! tell me what is best for my spiritual welfare; for I am Your disciple. Please direct me, I pray.

4 Lord of All Hearts: This epithet evokes the adorable aspect of Krishna, who, in his youth as a cowherd in the village of Brindaban, won the hearts of the cowherding girls *(gopis)* and boys *(gopas)*. Krishna is often called Govinda, meaning chief of the cowherds, which reflects his mastery of the senses (symbolized by cows).

5 Krishna's smile has been interpreted in several different ways. Some commentators think that Krishna is mocking Arjuna with his smile, but if we realize that Krishna, as a spiritual teacher, has only Arjuna's welfare at heart, we may envision the smile as an expression of grace, affection, or patient encouragement. Maharishi points out that although Arjuna is in despair, the Lord smiles in his usual playful mood to show Arjuna that his difficulties are not so serious as he thinks. Yogananda interprets the entire Gita as symbolic of internal experiences of the practitioner of yoga who is battling inner obstacles to liberation. He thus offers the image of Arjuna "basking in the illumining smile of Spirit" as he begins to receive Krishna's sublime discourse.

6 "Life is a series of experiences which need innumerable forms. Death is an interval in that one long life" (Meher Baba).

7 "Krishna is not speaking of the Stoic calmness, in which agitation of feeling is not outwardly expressed. The calmness of which He speaks is based on the knowledge of the Soul's immortality" (Nikhilananda).

8 "That which is not" is the ever-changing Nature (Prakriti); "that which is" is the eternal Spirit (Purusha in the Samkhya philosophy) or Self (Atman in Vedanta). "The ocean can exist without the waves, but the waves cannot manifest without the ocean. The ocean is the real substance, the waves are only temporary changes on the ocean, and therefore 'unreal' (in themselves they have no independent existence). The ocean, in essence, does not change whether it is calm or restless with waves; but the waves change their forms—they come and they go. Their essence is change, and therefore unreality" (Yogananda).

8 For should I attain the monarchy of the visible world, or over the invisible world, it would not drive away the anguish which is now paralyzing my senses.

Sanjaya continued:

9 Arjuna, the conqueror of all enemies, then told the Lord of All Hearts[4] that he would not fight, and became silent, O King!

10 Thereupon the Lord, with a gracious smile,[5] addressed him who was so much depressed in the midst between the two armies.

Lord Shri Krishna said:

11 Why grieve for those for whom no grief is due, and yet profess wisdom? The wise grieve neither for the dead nor for the living.

12 There was never a time when I was not, nor you, nor these princes were not; there will never be a time when we shall cease to be.

13 As the soul experiences in this body, infancy, youth, and old age, so finally it passes into another.[6] The wise have no delusion about this.

14 Those external relations which bring cold and heat, pain and happiness, they come and go; they are not permanent. Endure them bravely, O Prince!

15 The hero whose soul is unmoved by circumstance, who accepts pleasure and pain with equanimity,[7] only he is fit for immortality.

16 That which is not, shall never be; that which is, shall never cease to be.[8] To the wise, these truths are self-evident.

17 The Spirit, which pervades all that we see, is imperishable. Nothing can destroy the Spirit.

18 The material bodies which this Eternal, Indestructible, Immeasurable Spirit inhabits are all finite. Therefore fight, O Valiant Man!

19 He who thinks that the Spirit kills, and he who thinks of it as killed,

9 Verses 19–20 are quoted from the *Katha Upanishad* (1.2.19 and 1.2.18, respectively).

10 "He who is afraid kills. He for whom there is no death will not kill" (Gandhi).

11 Soldier: kshatriya, the caste of warriors and rulers. A righteous war is welcome because the duty *(svadharma)* of the soldier is to uphold justice and protect the people.

are both ignorant. The Spirit kills not, nor is it killed.

20 It was not born; It will never die: nor once having been, can It ever cease to be: Unborn, Eternal, Ever-enduring, yet Most Ancient, the Spirit dies not when the body is dead.[9]

21 He who knows the Spirit as Indestructible, Immortal, Unborn, Always-the-Same, how should he kill or cause to be killed?[10]

22 As a man discards his threadbare robes and puts on new, so the Spirit throws off Its worn-out bodies and takes fresh ones.

23 Weapons cleave It not, fire burns It not, water drenches It not, and wind dries It not.

24 It is impenetrable; It can be neither drowned nor scorched nor dried. It is Eternal, All-pervading, Unchanging, Immovable, and Most Ancient.

25 It is named the Unmanifest, the Unthinkable, the Immutable. Wherefore, knowing the Spirit as such, you have no cause to grieve.

26 Even if you think of it as constantly being born, constantly dying; even then, O Mighty Man! you still have no cause to grieve.

27 For death is as sure for that which is born as birth is for that which is dead. Therefore grieve not for what is inevitable.

28 The end and beginning of beings are unknown. We see only the intervening formations. Then what cause is there for grief?

29 One hears of the Spirit with surprise, another thinks It marvelous, the third listens without comprehending. Thus, though many are told about It, scarcely is there one who knows It.

30 Be not anxious about these armies. The Spirit in man is imperishable.

31 You must look at your duty. Nothing can be more welcome to a soldier than a righteous war.[11] Therefore to waver in your resolve is unworthy, O Arjuna!

12 Kunti is the mother of three of the five Pandava princes—Arjuna, Yudhishthira, and Bhima. (She is also Krishna's aunt.) Krishna often addresses Arjuna as Kaunteya, "son of Kunti." Since her sons are all great heroes, Krishna seems to be reminding Arjuna of his heroic status.

@ "The Gita is not a justification of war, nor does it propound a war-making mystique.... The Gita is saying that even in what appears 'unspiritual,' one can act with pure intentions and thus be guided by Krishna consciousness."

—Thomas Merton

13 The "philosophy of Knowledge" is Samkhya, one of six traditional systems of Indian philosophy; elsewhere it is referred to as *jnana yoga*. Among its teachings is the distinction between soul and body explained by Krishna above. It also stresses renunciation of action.

14 The "philosophy of Action" is Yoga, specifically *karma yoga*, which stresses renunciation of the fruits of action but not of action itself.

@ The various schools of philosophy need not be seen as competing with one another: "Sankhya and Yoga are never at daggers drawn. One is detached meditative knowledge, and the other is dedicated and selfless action. They have the self-same Goal. They just follow two different paths to arrive at the Goal."

—Sri Chinmoy

15 Figurative: literally "flowery." The ignorant are attached to words and think there is nothing in the Vedas but rituals for attaining heaven, wealth, and the like; they ignore the teachings that lead to liberation.

32   Blessed are the soldiers who find their opportunity. This opportunity has opened for you the gates of heaven.

33   Refuse to fight in this righteous cause, and you will be a traitor, lost to fame, incurring only sin.

34   Men will talk forever of your disgrace; and to the noble, dishonor is worse than death.

35   Great generals will think that you have fled from the battlefield through cowardice; though once honored, you will seem despicable.

36   Your enemies will spread scandal and mock at your courage. Can anything be more humiliating?

37   If killed, you shall attain heaven; if victorious, enjoy the kingdom of earth. Therefore arise, O son of Kunti![12] and fight.

38   Look upon pleasure and pain, victory and defeat, with an equal eye. Make ready for the combat, and you shall commit no sin.

39   I have told you the philosophy of Knowledge.[13] Now listen! and I will explain the philosophy of Action,[14] by means of which, O Arjuna, you shall break through the bondage of all action.

40   On this Path, endeavor is never wasted, nor can it ever be repressed. Even a very little of its practice protects one from great danger.

41   By its means, the straying intellect becomes steadied in the contemplation of one object only; whereas the minds of the irresolute stray into bypaths innumerable.

42   Only the ignorant speak in figurative[15] language. It is they who extol the letter of the scriptures, saying, "There is nothing deeper than this."

43   Consulting only their desires, they construct their own heaven, devising arduous and complex rites to secure their own pleasure and their own power; and the only result is rebirth.

16 | Vedic Scriptures: *Rig Veda* (verses and songs in praise of the gods),
Sama Veda (chants), *Yajur Veda* (a priestly manual for performing rituals of sacrifice), and *Atharva Veda* (magic formulas).

17 | In Sanskrit, the first of the three Qualities *(gunas)* is *sattva,* called
Purity in this version (other translators render it as goodness, consciousness, or truth). *Rajas* is Passion (desire, attachment, activity, the dynamic principle), and *tamas* is Ignorance (inertia, darkness).

The doctrine of the three Qualities is found in the Vedas, which
prescribe rituals for those who, under the influence of the Qualities,
seek to attain material rewards and blessings of the gods. Such rituals
are the very opposite of what Krishna is teaching about action without concern for reward. So, in telling Arjuna to rise above the Qualities,
Krishna seems also to say that the spiritual seeker ultimately has to go
beyond the conventions of rites, rituals, and scriptures.

18 | Other translators interpret this verse to mean that an enlightened
person has no need for scriptures, just as there is no need for a well
when the whole countryside is flooded. "The state of realization is like
a reservoir full of water, from which people quite naturally draw to
satisfy all their needs instead of getting their water from many small
ponds. Therefore the Lord asks Arjuna to 'be without the three gunas'
and not waste his life in planning and achieving small gains in the
ever-changing field of the three gunas" (Maharishi).

19 | Pure Intelligence: *buddhi yoga,* "taking refuge in the 'wisdom-faculty'"
(Feuerstein). On *buddhi,* see below, n. 27.

20 | Contemplation of the Infinite: *samadhi,* a state of consciousness
equated with ecstatic concentration on the object of meditation, so
that all mental activity stops.

21 | "Spirituality" is Purohit Swami's translation of the word *yoga,* which
signifies the state of union with God as well as any of several paths or
disciplines that lead to union. The physical discipline known as *hatha
yoga* is the best-known yoga in the West, but many regard it as only a
preliminary path leading to more advanced practices.

44 While their minds are absorbed with ideas of power and personal enjoyment, they cannot concentrate their discrimination on one point.

45 The Vedic Scriptures[16] tell of the three constituents of life—the Qualities.[17] Rise above all of them, O Arjuna! above all the pairs of opposing sensations; be steady in truth, free from worldly anxieties, and centered in the Self.

46 As a man can drink water from any side of a full tank, so the skilled theologian can wrest from any scripture that which will serve his purpose.[18]

47 But you have only the right to work; but none to the fruit thereof. Let not then the fruit of your action be your motive; nor yet be enamored of inaction.

48 Perform all your actions with mind concentrated on the Divine, renouncing attachment and looking upon success and failure with an equal eye. Spirituality implies equanimity.

49 Physical action is far inferior to an intellect concentrated on the Divine. Have recourse then to the Pure Intelligence.[19] It is only the petty-minded who work for reward.

50 When a man attains to Pure Reason, he renounces in this world the results of good and evil alike. Cling to Right Action. Spirituality is the real art of living.

51 The sages guided by Pure Intellect renounce the fruit of action; and, freed from the chains of rebirth, they reach the highest bliss.

52 When your reason has crossed the entanglements of illusion, then shall you become indifferent both to the philosophies you have heard and to those you may yet hear.

53 When the intellect, bewildered by the multiplicity of holy scripts, stands unperturbed in blissful contemplation of the Infinite,[20] then have you attained Spirituality.[21]

22 "This question of Arjuna's introduces the glorious eighteen stanzas [55–72] which, as Gandhi points out, hold the key to the interpretation of the entire Bhagavad Gita. Gandhi, a devoted student of the Gita, was especially drawn to these last eighteen verses of the second chapter…. In every verse of this passage we have clear proof that the battle referred to is within, between the forces of selfishness and the forces of selflessness, between the ferocious pull of the senses and the serene tranquility of spiritual wisdom. I strongly recommend these verses to be memorized for use in meditation because they gradually can bring about the transformation of our consciousness" (Easwaran).

23 Accepts good and evil alike: This means that one does not get overexcited when good things happen or upset when bad things happen. It does not imply that one invites or sanctions evil. As Ramakrishna said, God is in everything—but you do not embrace a tiger.

24 The tortoise image is a favorite metaphor for the practice of *pratyahara*, withdrawal of the senses or the "ability to free sense activity from the domination of external objects" (Eliade). "The senses can be involved with outer experiences and yet not be totally engrossed in them to the extent that they transfer to the mind impressions deep enough to become the seed of future desires" (Maharishi).

25 Mind: *manas*, here meaning the lower mind, which receives impressions from the senses and relays them to the higher mind (*buddhi*; see n. 27). The function of *manas* includes both thought and emotion.

26 Desire *(kama)* is said to breed anger because anger arises when desire is thwarted.

27 Reason: *buddhi*, rendered elsewhere as "intelligence" or "intellect," the seat of wisdom *(jnana, vidya, prajna)*. The word comes from the root *bud*, "to awaken." "Buddhi is the aspect of consciousness that is filled with light and reveals the truth. When one's Buddhi becomes fully developed, one becomes a Buddha, or enlightened one. The main action of intelligence is to discern the true and real from the false and unreal" (Frawley).

Arjuna asked:

54 My Lord! How can we recognize the saint who has attained Pure Intellect, who has reached this state of Bliss, and whose mind is steady? How does he talk, how does he live, and how does he act?[22]

Lord Shri Krishna replied:

55 When a man has given up the desires of his heart and is satisfied with the Self alone, be sure that he has reached the highest state.

56 The sage, whose mind is unruffled in suffering, whose desire is not roused by enjoyment, who is without attachment, anger, or fear—take him to be one who stands at that lofty level.

57 He who, wherever he goes, is attached to no person and to no place by ties of flesh; who accepts good and evil alike,[23] neither welcoming the one nor shrinking from the other—take him to be one who is merged in the Infinite.

58 He who can withdraw his senses from the attraction of their objects, as the tortoise draws his limbs within his shell[24]—take it that such a one has attained Perfection.

59 The objects of sense turn from him who is abstemious. Even the relish for them is lost in him who has seen the Truth.

60 O Arjuna! The mind[25] of him who is trying to conquer it is forcibly carried away in spite of his efforts, by his tumultuous senses.

61 Restraining them all, let him meditate steadfastly on Me; for who thus conquers his senses achieves perfection.

62 When a man dwells on the objects of sense, he creates an attraction for them; attraction develops into desire, and desire breeds anger.[26]

63 Anger induces delusion; delusion, loss of memory; through loss of memory, reason[27] is shattered; and loss of reason leads to destruction.

28 Eternal peace: *prasada*, serenity or clarity. *Prasada* also means "grace." Srila Prabhupada translates it in this verse as "the complete mercy of the Lord." By the grace or mercy of God, the devotee becomes liberated from delusion.

29 Reason: *prajna*. See above, n. 27.

30 Saint: *muni*, "silent one." A *muni* is an advanced aspirant who has reached a high level of consciousness through practicing austerities such as silence. The English word *saint* has specific associations in Christianity. In this translation, a more general sense of spiritual holiness seems to be intended.

31 Self, Supreme Spirit: Brahman, the ultimate Reality, the formless absolute state of God, which is inseparable from the personal God and also identical with the soul or inmost self (Atman) of every being. Brahman is all, the One without a second. Because it cannot be described, it is often referred to by negation: *neti, neti*, "not this, not that."

32 "Become one with the Eternal": literally, "reach the *nirvana* of Brahman." *Nirvana* means "blown out," like a candle, but it is not utter extinction or a state of nonbeing; Sri Easwaran explains it as the extinction of the limited, selfish personality. The illusion of separate individuality ceases to exist when the self merges with Brahman, just as the limited nature of a drop of seawater disappears when it reunites with the ocean.

@ "One of the beauties of the Bhagavad Gita is that it does not say 'You should do this' or 'You shouldn't do that.' Sri Krishna simply says that if you want joy, security, wisdom, then this is the path. If you want sorrow, insecurity, and despair, then that is the path. He gives both maps in graphic detail, and tells you that it is for you to decide where you want to go."

—Eknath Easwaran

64 But the self-controlled soul, who moves among sense objects free from either attachment or repulsion, he wins eternal peace.[28]

65 Having attained peace, he becomes free from misery; for when the mind gains peace, right discrimination follows.

66 Right discrimination is not for him who cannot concentrate. Without concentration, there cannot be meditation; he who cannot meditate must not expect peace; and without peace, how can anyone expect happiness?

67 As a ship at sea is tossed by the tempest, so the reason[29] is carried away by the mind when preyed upon by the straying senses.

68 Therefore, O Mighty-in-Arms! he who keeps his senses detached from their objects—take it that his reason is purified.

69 The saint[30] is awake when the world sleeps, and he ignores that for which the world lives.

70 He attains peace into whom desires flow as rivers into the ocean, which though brimming with water remains ever the same; not he whom desire carries away.

71 He attains peace who, giving up desire, moves through the world without aspiration, possessing nothing which he can call his own, and free from pride.

72 O Arjuna! This is the state of the Self, the Supreme Spirit,[31] to which if a man once attain, it shall never be taken from him. Even at the time of leaving the body, he will remain firmly enthroned there, and will become one with the Eternal.[32]

1 Freedom from activity: *naishkarmya*, the calm state of "actionless action" enjoyed by those who are without desire. Such persons may not be active in the world, but their very presence helps others. However, *naishkarmya* does not necessarily mean inactivity; it means action free from the binding sense of oneself as the doer. "The objective of spiritual advancement is not so much 'works' but the quality of life free from ego-consciousness" (Meher Baba).

☐ The Path of Action:
Karma Yoga

Arjuna questioned:

1 My Lord! If wisdom is above action, why do you advise me to engage in this terrible fight?

2 Your language perplexes me and confuses my reason. Therefore please tell me the only way by which I may, without doubt, secure my spiritual welfare.

Lord Shri Krishna replied:

3 In this world, as I have said, there is a twofold path, O Sinless One! There is the Path of Wisdom for those who meditate and the Path of Action for those who work.

4 No man can attain freedom from activity[1] by refraining from action, nor can one reach perfection by merely refusing to act.

5 He cannot even for a moment remain really inactive; for the Qualities of Nature will compel him to act whether he will or no.

6 Whoever remains motionless, refusing to act, but all the while brooding over sensuous objects, that deluded soul is simply a hypocrite.

7 But, O Arjuna! All honor to him whose mind controls his senses; for he is thereby beginning to practice Karma Yoga, the Path of Right Action, keeping himself always unattached.

8 Do your duty as prescribed; for action for duty's sake is superior to inaction. Even the maintenance of the body would be impossible if one remained inactive.

2 | Sacrifice: *yajna*. Literally, this word refers to ancient Vedic oblations offered to the sacred fire. Its inner meaning is any action done with self-giving love, free from ego-consciousness, with the motive of pleasing the Lord; "an offering of oneself, one's being, one's mind, heart, will, body, life, actions to the Divine" (Aurobindo).

@ | "Let us give up our whole body and mind and everything as an eternal sacrifice unto the Lord and be at peace, perfect peace, with ourselves. Instead of pouring oblations into the fire, as in a sacrifice, perform this one great sacrifice day and night—the sacrifice of your little self. 'I searched for wealth in this world; Thou art the only wealth I have found; I sacrifice myself unto Thee. I searched for someone to love; Thou art the only beloved I have found; I sacrifice myself unto Thee.'"

—Swami Vivekananda

3 | The entire universe was created from the sacrifice of the gigantic body of the Cosmic Person, known as Purusha or Prajapati (the Creator of *praja*, human beings). The principle of sacrifice thus plays an essential role from the very beginning of life to its ultimate goal, God-Realization. Through *yajna*, life flourishes and bears fruit.

4 | Powers of Nature: *devas*, literally "shining ones," often translated as "gods." The *devas* are divine beings equated with the forces of nature and are distinct from the one supreme God. They represent certain "offices" that are filled successively by various souls. But although they may dwell in the heavenly realms, they are neither immortal nor spiritually perfect. Spiritual perfection can only be attained in human form.

9 In this world people are fettered by action, unless it is performed as a sacrifice.**2** Therefore, O Arjuna! let your acts be done without attachment, as sacrifice only.

10 In the beginning, when God created all beings by the sacrifice of Himself, He said unto them: "Through sacrifice you can procreate, and it shall satisfy all your desires.**3**

11 "Worship the Powers of Nature**4** thereby, and let them nourish you in return; thus supporting each other, you shall attain your highest welfare.

12 "For, fed on sacrifice, Nature will give you all the enjoyment you can desire. But whoever enjoys what she gives without returning is, indeed, a robber."

13 The sages who enjoy the food that remains after the sacrifice is made are freed from all sin; but the selfish who spread their feast only for themselves feed on sin only.

14 All creatures are the product of food, food is the product of rain, rain comes by sacrifice, and sacrifice is the noblest form of action.

15 All action originates in the Supreme Spirit, which is Imperishable, and in sacrificial action the all-pervading Spirit is consciously present.

16 Thus he who does not help the revolving wheel of sacrifice, but instead leads a sinful life, rejoicing in the gratification of his senses, O Arjuna! he breathes in vain.

17 On the other hand, the soul who meditates on the Self, is content to serve the Self, and rests satisfied within the Self—there remains nothing more for him to accomplish.

18 He has nothing to gain by the performance or nonperformance of action. His welfare depends not on any contribution that an earthly creature can make.

19 Therefore do your duty perfectly, without care for the results; for he who does his duty disinterestedly attains the Supreme.

5 King Janaka was an enlightened ruler and the father of Sita, heroine of the epic *Ramayana*. He continued to be active in the world even after attaining perfection, for the sake of "enlightening the world": *loka-samgraha*. This famous phrase from the Gita literally means "world gathering" or harmonizing the world. To help others toward enlightenment is the highest form of selfless service. The ideal of *loka-samgraha* is the basis of the Mahayana Buddhist path of the bodhisattva.

6 Personal egotism: *ahamkara*, the consciousness of "I." The activity of this organ of self-consciousness creates the illusion of the self as separate from God and causes us to identify ourselves as the agent of action. Ramana Maharshi (1879–1950) taught meditation on the question "Who am I?" as a means of uprooting this identification with the false ego.

@ "There are two types of ego. The false ego has innumerable wants and desires. It says, I am a man, I want this; I am a woman, I want that; I am sick; I want to be happy; I am rich; I am very poor.... It is always 'I.' But when this ego is annihilated, a transformation takes place: the false 'I' is replaced by the real 'I,' and the experience, 'I am free from desires and wanting, I am infinite, I am one with God,' is gained. That is the Real Ego."   —Meher Baba

7 "This injunction of the Gita does not mean that a saint should not awaken people at all; they should be gradually roused, and instructed in higher principles only when they are receptive—when they begin to wonder about the mysteries of life, either as a result of introspective thinking or of worldly misfortune and material disillusionment" (Yogananda).

8 Surrendering: that is, dedicating one's every action to God and leaving to him the responsibility for its results.

9 Bondage of all action: a reference to the natural law of karma (Sanskrit *karman*). By this law, whatever we are and whatever we do is the consequence of impressions *(samskaras)* deposited in the mental body by our thoughts, words, and deeds of past lives. These impressions,

20 King Janaka[5] and others attained perfection through action alone. Even for the sake of enlightening the world, it is your duty to act;

21 For whatever a great man does, others imitate. People conform to the standard which he has set.

22 There is nothing in this universe, O Arjuna! that I am compelled to do; nor anything for Me to attain; yet I am persistently active.

23 For were I not to act without ceasing, O Prince! people would be glad to do likewise.

24 And if I were to refrain from action, the human race would be ruined; I should lead the world to chaos, and destruction would follow.

25 As the ignorant act because of their fondness for action, so should the wise act without such attachment, fixing their eyes, O Arjuna! only on the welfare of the world.

26 But a wise man should not perturb the minds of the ignorant, who are attached to action; let him perform his own actions in the right spirit, with concentration on Me, thus inspiring all to do the same.

27 Action is the product of the Qualities inherent in Nature. It is only the ignorant man who, misled by personal egotism,[6] says: "I am the doer."

28 But he, O Mighty One! who understands correctly the relation of the Qualities to action is not attached to the act, for he perceives that it is merely the action and reaction of the Qualities among themselves.

29 Those who do not understand the Qualities are interested in the act. Still, the wise man who knows the truth should not disturb the mind of him who does not.[7]

30 Therefore, surrendering[8] your actions unto Me, your thoughts concentrated on the Absolute, free from selfishness and without anticipation of reward, with mind devoid of excitement, begin to fight.

31 Those who act always in accordance with My precepts, firm in faith and without caviling, they too are freed from the bondage of action.[9]

carried in latent form into our next life, determine our future temperament and destiny. Just as one can be bound by a chain of gold or a chain of iron, so good as well as bad actions can bind us spiritually. But, as Meher Baba explains: "Good as well as bad karma binds as long as it feeds the ego-mind through wrong understanding. But karma becomes a power for Emancipation when it springs from right understanding and wears out the ego-mind."

10 In one sense, our own duty (svadharma) is the activity appropriate to our station in life. Whatever work happens to be our lot in life might be considered our duty. More broadly, it is our life purpose, an ideal to which we are inwardly called. If we follow the path suited to our own nature, we will make good progress; but if we try to imitate someone else's path, we are in danger of falling back. Such a loss would be worse than death, which after all is "only a temporary pause in the process of evolution. A pause like this is no real danger to life because, with a new body taken after the pause, more rapid progress in life evolution becomes possible" (Maharishi). The safest and most effective path, then, is one's own duty, even if performed imperfectly or unsuccessfully—as long as we work honestly, at activities that do not harm others, and leave the results to God.

@ "Any action that makes us go Godward is a good action and is our duty; any action that makes us go downward is evil and is not our duty."

—Swami Vivekananda

11 Wanting pleasure and wishing to avoid pain are two sides of the same coin; both attraction and aversion are born of desire.

12 Mind: manas. Reason: buddhi.

13 "He" refers here to God, the indwelling Supreme Self. "He, the Self, the witness of reason, is superior to reason" (Shankara).

32 But they who ridicule My word and do not keep it are ignorant, devoid of wisdom, and blind. They seek but their own destruction.

33 Even the wise man acts in character with his nature; indeed, all creatures act according to their natures. What is the use of compulsion then?

34 The love and hate which are aroused by the objects of sense arise from Nature; do not yield to them. They only obstruct the path.

35 It is better to do your own duty,[10] however lacking in merit, than to do that of another, even though efficiently. It is better to die doing one's own duty, for to do the duty of another is fraught with danger.

Arjuna asked:

36 My Lord! Tell me, what is it that drives a man to sin, even against his will and as if by compulsion?

Lord Shri Krishna said:

37 It is desire, it is aversion, born of passion.[11] Desire consumes and corrupts everything. It is man's greatest enemy.

38 As fire is shrouded in smoke, a mirror by dust, and a child by the womb, so is the universe enveloped in desire.

39 It is the wise man's constant enemy; it tarnishes the face of wisdom. It is as insatiable as a flame of fire.

40 It works through the senses, the mind, and the reason,[12] and with their help destroys wisdom and confounds the soul.

41 Therefore, O Arjuna! first control your senses, and then slay desire; for it is full of sin, and is the destroyer of knowledge and of wisdom.

42 It is said that the senses are powerful. But beyond the senses is the mind, beyond mind is intellect, and beyond and greater than intellect is He.[13]

43 Thus, O Mighty-in-Arms! knowing him to be beyond the intellect and, by His help, subduing your personal egotism, kill your enemy, Desire, extremely difficult though it be.

1 "The vast masses of mankind are content with material things; but there are some who are awake and want to get back, who have had enough of this playing here. These struggle consciously, while the rest do it unconsciously" (Vivekananda). "We should look upon ourselves as those exceptional persons among thousands" (Gandhi).

2 Ether: *akasha*, all-pervasive space, the finest of the five elements.

3 Mind, intellect, and personality: *manas, buddhi,* and *ahamkara.*

4 Manifested Nature: Prakriti. See "The Philosophy of Discrimination," n. 8, p. 18.

5 "Contemplating matter, the soul becomes entangled in the world; contemplating the Spirit, it attains liberation. Hence the Spirit-form of the Lord is superior to His matter-form" (Nikhilananda).

6 Worlds created and dissolved: the cyclic dissolution *(pralaya)* of the universe.

7 OM: This sacred syllable, expressive of the highest cosmic consciousness, may be called a mantra (sacred utterance), a name of God, or a primordial creative vibration that pervades the universe. It is described as an approximation of the "sound of the soundless Absolute." The word appears at the beginning of written works and may be uttered at the beginning and end of a prayer or recitation from the scriptures. The kinship of OM with the Hebrew *amen* and Arabic *amin* ("so be it") is pointed out by Meher Baba, who adds, "Coming from a man, 'So be it' is a blessing or a wish; but coming from God it is creation." Yogananda also links OM to the Tibetan mantra HUM.

OM is sometimes spelled AUM, because it is made up of three sounds

☐ Knowledge and Experience

Lord Shri Krishna said:

1 Listen, O Arjuna! And I will tell you how you shall know Me in My full perfection, practicing meditation with your mind devoted to Me, and having Me for your refuge.

2 I will reveal this knowledge unto you, and how it may be realized; which, once accomplished, there remains nothing else worth having in this life.

3 Among thousands of people, scarcely one strives for perfection,[1] and even among those who gain occult powers, perchance but one knows Me in truth.

4 Earth, water, fire, air, ether,[2] mind, intellect, and personality[3]—this is the eightfold division of My Manifested Nature.[4]

5 This is My inferior Nature; but distinct from this, O Valiant One! know that My Superior Nature is the very Life which sustains the universe.[5]

6 It is the womb of all being; for I am He by whom the worlds were created and shall be dissolved.[6]

7 O Arjuna! There is nothing higher than Me; all is strung upon Me as rows of pearls upon a thread.

8 O Arjuna! I am the Fluidity in water, the Light in the sun and in the moon. I am the mystic syllable Om[7] in the Vedic scriptures, the Sound in ether, the Virility in man.

9 I am the Fragrance of earth, the Brilliance of fire. I am the Life Force in all beings, and I am the Austerity of the ascetics.

(the letter *o* consisting of the sounds *a* and *u*), which, respectively, are compared to three states of consciousness: waking (equated with the gross realm of manifestation), dreaming (subtle), and sleeping (causal). The syllable as a whole indicates a fourth state (*turiya,* "fourth")—the state of the transcendental Self.

8 Attachment: *raga.* Desire: *kama.*

9 Although desire is the enemy, the desire for truth or righteousness *(dharma)* is the one desire that eventually ends all desire. "The only Real Desire is to see God, and the only Real Longing is to become one with God. This Real Desire and Longing frees one from the bondage of birth and death. Other desires and longings bind one with ignorance" (Meher Baba).

10 "It is like a mirage in the desert. From the standpoint of the onlooker, the illusory water exists in the desert; but the desert does not depend upon or exist in the mirage. Likewise the universe, apparently superimposed on the Lord, exists in the Lord, but the Lord is not in the universe" (Nikhilananda).

11 Divine Illusion: Maya, the creative power that makes the illusory world of duality appear real; "the deluding cosmic hypnosis" (Yogananda). In the Gita, Maya is identified with Nature (Prakriti) and the three Qualities. Although it creates the false illusion of the finite world, in itself it is "divine in its power and therefore difficult to overcome" (Ramanuja). An aspect of the Goddess, Maya is inscrutable. Jnanadeva says: "Maya both is and is not. She is as impossible to describe as the child of a barren woman…. Only through her does the splendor of the Supreme become manifest."

"Even though the Lord manifests through maya, the tangible relative universe, and appears to be its cause and support, yet He is always One and without a second, transcendental, incorporeal, and unattached. This is His eternal mystery" (Nikhilananda). This paradox of the ultimate Reality was often alluded to by Sri Ramana Maharshi by quoting a well-known saying attributed to Shankara: "The world is illusory; Brahman alone is real; Brahman is the world."

10 Know, O Arjuna! that I am the eternal Seed of being; I am the Intelligence of the intelligent, the Splendor of the resplendent.

11 I am the Strength of the strong, of them who are free from attachment and desire;[8] and, O Arjuna! I am the Desire for righteousness.[9]

12 Whatever be the nature of their life, whether it be Pure or Passionate or Ignorant, they all are derived from Me. They are in Me, but I am not in them.[10]

13 The inhabitants of this world, misled by those natures which the Qualities have engendered, know not that I am higher than them all, and that I do not change.

14 Verily, this Divine Illusion[11] of Phenomena manifesting itself in the Qualities is difficult to surmount. Only they who devote themselves to Me and to Me alone can accomplish it.

15 The sinner, the ignorant, the vile, deprived of spiritual perception by the glamour of Illusion, and he who pursues a godless life—none of them shall find Me.

16 O Arjuna! The righteous who worship Me are grouped by stages: first they who suffer, next they who desire knowledge, then they who thirst after truth, and lastly they who attain wisdom.

17 Of all these, he who has gained wisdom, who meditates on Me without ceasing, devoting himself only to Me, he is the best; for by the wise man I am exceedingly beloved, and the wise man, too, is beloved by Me.

18 Noble-minded are they all, but the wise man I hold as my own Self; for he, remaining always at peace with Me, makes Me his final goal.

19 After many lives, at last the wise man realizes Me as I am. A man so enlightened that he sees God everywhere is very difficult to find.

20 They in whom wisdom is obscured by one desire or the other worship the lesser Powers, practicing many rites, which vary according to their temperaments.

12 In India it is customary to worship the form *(murti)* of a deity—for example, to place food, fruits, and flowers before an image of Krishna, or to pray or meditate before it. Even just viewing a divine form (an act known as *darshana*, "sight, vision")—whether it is a statue, a painting, or the living presence of a spiritually perfect person—"is an act of worship, and through the eyes one gains the blessing of the divine" (Eck). However, although meditation on the form of a deity or a perfect one helps the aspirant to absorb divine qualities into his or her own being, it is unwise to overemphasize the physical form. The body of Krishna was merely a coat that he put on to make himself visible to the world. One must strive to see the Avatar as he really is, in his all-pervading infinite being—which in reality is our own Self. "He who worships God merely as a finite form will not attain the transcendental divine union with His infinite nature" (Yogananda).

@ "Age after age the infinite God wills through His infinite mercy to come among mankind by descending to the human level in a human form. His physical presence among mankind is not understood and He is looked upon as an ordinary man of the world. When He asserts His divinity by proclaiming Himself the Avatar of the age, He is worshipped by some who accept Him as God, and glorified by a few who know him as God on earth. It happens invariably, though, that the rest of humanity condemns Him while He is physically among them."

—Meher Baba

13 The life of the world: Adhibhuta, that which underlies all the elements.

14 The universal sacrifice: Adhiyajna, the lord of sacrifice.

15 Pure Divinity: Adhidaiva, that which underlies all the gods.

21 But whatever the form of worship, if the devotee have faith, then upon his faith in that worship do I set My own seal.

22 If he worships one form alone with real faith, then shall his desires be fulfilled through that only; for thus have I ordained.

23 The fruit that comes to men of limited insight is, after all, finite. They who worship the Lower Powers attain them; but those who worship Me come unto Me alone.

24 The ignorant think of Me, who am the Unmanifested Spirit, as if I were really in human form. They do not understand that My Supreme Nature is changeless and most excellent.[12]

25 I am not visible to all, for I am enveloped by the Illusion of Phenomena. This deluded world does not know Me as the Unborn and the Imperishable.

26 I know, O Arjuna! all beings in the past, the present, and the future; but they do not know Me.

27 O brave Arjuna! Man lives in a fairy world, deceived by the glamour of opposite sensations, infatuated by desire and aversion.

28 But those who act righteously, in whom sin has been destroyed, who are free from the infatuation of the conflicting emotions, they worship Me with firm resolution.

29 Those who make Me their refuge, who strive for liberation from decay and death, they realize the Supreme Spirit, which is their own real Self, and in which all action finds its consummation.

30 Those who see Me in the life of the world,[13] in the universal sacrifice,[14] and as pure Divinity,[15] keeping their minds steady, they live in Me, even in the crucial hour of death.

2 ■ Buddha

The Buddha

Painting by Narayan Chitrakar

Walking with Buddha ☐

In the *Anguttara Nikaya,* one of the oldest of the Pali Buddhist scriptures (and part of what is known as "The Third Basket of Discourses," the *Sutta Pitaka*), there is a haunting portrait of the Buddha. One day, a Hindu priest found the Buddha sitting under a tree in a state of deep peace: "His faculties were at rest, his mind was still and everything around him breathed self-discipline and serenity." The Buddha reminded the priest of an old male elephant; there was the same sense of great power being controlled and channeled into a force of gentleness.

The Brahman was amazed and asked the Buddha, "Are you a god?" "No," the Buddha answered. "Are you becoming an angel...or a spirit?" Once again, the Buddha replied that he was not; everything that limited him to a human existence of suffering had been, he said, "cut off at the root, chopped off like a palm stump done away with." The Buddha compared himself to a red lotus that had begun its life underwater but now rose above the water's surface. "So I too was born and grew up in the world, but I have transcended the world and I am no longer touched by it."

He had attained nirvana. Through dying to his false self and devoting his entire life to the unstinting service of others, the Buddha had freed himself to live in the vivid serenity and spaciousness of a consciousness beyond struggle and suffering. The priest plucked up his courage once more and asked the Buddha how, then, he should be categorized. "Remember me," the Buddha said quietly, "as someone who has woken up."

The confidence, clarity, and calm splendor of the Buddha's presence, as described in the *Anguttara Nikaya,* permeate the Dhammapada. Although monks compiled and edited this text about a hundred years after the Buddha's death and may have doctored it for polemical purposes, anyone reading the Dhammapada seriously and consistently has an overwhelming sense of the spiritual personality behind its teachings—a personality at once austere, forthright, and profoundly compassionate. The Buddha was both deeply troubled by the suffering, anguish, and evil in the world and also certain of the path that leads to overcoming and transcending them. In the section "Old Age," the Buddha appears to be directly and personally describing his own spiritual realization—the same realization the Hindu priest felt so richly, and from whose luminous silence and authority all of the words of the Dhammapada's teachings flow, and in whose shining they are all bathed:

> Looking for the maker of this house, I ran to no avail through a string of many births, and wearisome is birth again and again. But now, maker of the house, you have been seen. You shall not raise this house again. All the rafters are broken; the ridgepole is shattered. The mind, approaching eternity, has attained the extinction of all desires.

My own relationship with the message and truths of the Dhammapada has had three distinct stages, which I suspect mirror the progressive understanding of many modern seekers grappling with this seminal and always challenging text.

In the first stage, my admiration for the Buddha and his teachings was uncritical. I was in awe of the Buddha's spiritual prestige and profoundly moved by his pragmatic radicalism; his desire to teach the highest truths to everyone in a popular language; his refusal of all superstition, pseudo-mystical "explanations," and cultic rituals; and his relentlessly honest insistence on a rigorous, disciplined, self-responsible path to awakening. At the time I first studied the Dhammapada in depth, I was making a pilgrimage to the Buddhist sites in northern India. Three statements from the Dhammapada became the focus and inspiration of my journey:

> All that we are is the result of what we have thought.

> Through meditation, wisdom is won. Through lack of meditation, wisdom is lost.

Your own self is your master. Who else could it be? With self well subdued, you gain a master hard to find.

The no-nonsense force of these statements—as well as their wisdom—delighted me. Reading from the Dhammapada in the Indian cities of Bodh Gaya and Sarnath, and in buses and trains along the way, I was struck again and again by the earthiness of the way in which the Buddha taught the highest truths. Like Jesus, Ramakrishna, and Muhammad, the Buddha had a genius for illustrating the most elevated concepts with the simplest imaginable images and metaphors:

The evil done by one's self, born of one's self, suckled by one's self, crushes the foolish including oneself, even as a diamond cuts a stone.

If a fool is associated with a wise person for an entire lifetime, that fool will perceive the truth as little as a spoon perceives the taste of soup.

I had been brought up in the European tradition of irony and fierce psychological analysis; the Buddha's hardheaded transcendental realism, so graphic and naked in its transmission, spoke to me directly, in a way that some of the Hindu mystical texts, with their recondite language and baroque ecstasies, could not.

Fifteen years later, in light of both my own inner revolution in mystical consciousness and an intensive study of the Divine Feminine in all traditions, I found myself taking a more critical look at the Buddha's teachings. My inner experience of the Mother-aspect of God and of the sacredness of the immanent and created world—and my increasing distress at how the Sacred Feminine had been degraded or betrayed in all of the major mystical and religious transmissions systems—led me to read the Dhammapada in a different light.

I came to understand how rooted in his own autobiographical experience the Buddha's teachings were. They reflected and enshrined as law the circumstances of his own awakening, which took the form of a very "masculine" rejection of home, marriage, sexuality, and householder responsibility in favor of a heroic search beyond the confines of relationship or society.

I became conscious of what I called an "addiction to transcendence"—and a kind of unconscious dualism that resulted from it, even in mystical philosophies that seemed to celebrate the unity of reality—running through all of the spirituality of the first axial age (the age from the seventh to the third centuries B.C.E. when a new spirituality flowered in China, India, and Greece). How could any philosophy that rejected much of earth life and a great deal of the feminine authentically reflect divine unity?

In this second stage of my reading of the Dhammapada, I never lost my awe for the Buddha or my joy at what had first moved me in his teachings. What I became aware of, however, was a slant that showed itself in body-hatred, fear of sex, fear of women, an obsession with emotional detachment, and an almost exclusive privileging of celibacy and solitude as the one way of life that could lead to illumination. The Buddhist scholars I spoke to at length about this either side-stepped the questions I raised ("They are not really important in the overall vision"), historicized them ("How could the Buddha not have been slightly patriarchal given his time?"), or dismissed the passages in which an antifeminist stance occurs as "polemical implants" of later monks anxious to claim the Buddha's authority for their own ascetic path.

Explaining away important issues surrounding the denial or denigration of the Sacred Feminine in the Dhammapada—and by implication in the whole range of the Buddha's teachings—does not serve either the interest of truth or the Buddha's own realization. Didn't the Awakened One enjoin us to take nothing on trust, even from him, and to test his statements in the crucible of our own experience? Didn't the Buddha say on several occasions that his teachings were to be used as a raft to get to the other shore, to be discarded or modified when the truth had been reached? To imply that the teachings of the Buddha, as set forth in the Dhammapada, have limitations is not to deny their grandeur or truth; rather, it is to expand them to embrace kinds of truth and approaches to creation that we now see clearly are essential to the survival of a human race.

We are living through, I believe, a second axial age in which the patri-archal distortions of the first have to be corrected and filled out in all the mystical and religious transmission systems. The keys to the effectiveness of the second axial age is the restoration of the full dignity and power of the Sacred Feminine, so that the "sacred marriage" of masculine and fem-inine, transcendence and immanence, clarity and passion, and wisdom and compassion can take place within every human being and engender a divinized humanity capable at last of co-creating with the Divine a trans-formed world.

A careful look at the Dhammapada, however, reveals just how persua-sive the denial is of everything associated with the feminine and creation: "This body is a painted image, covered with wounds, bunched together, sickly, weak, and impermanent.... This heap of corruption falls to pieces, life ending in death." In the Buddha's description of creation, he stresses its illusory nature: "Look upon the world as you would on a bubble. Look upon it as a mirage." While it is true that all reality reveals itself as a play of Light to one whose consciousness has become aware of the Light, this does not mean that reality is a mirage. All it means is that the reality our untransformed senses have registered is illusory. "True" reality is not unreal but super-real, utterly saturated with divine presence, the epiphany of divine beauty and truth. The Buddha's beliefs about the emptiness of the real world and its illusoriness are partly dictated by a pessimism about matter and the world. It is this largely unexamined pessimism that under-lies his description of life ("There is no pain like this bodily existence.... Bodily demands are the greatest of evils") and his understanding of enlightenment as a state of removal from and of the world ("Give up what is ahead, give up what is behind, give up what is between, when you go to the other shore of existence").

My reading of the Dhammapada now has entered a third stage, one that unites and fuses the admiration of my first encounter with the critical understanding I have explored here. Once I saw and accepted the patriar-chal distortion in the Buddha's teachings and saw how they can color and limit the vision of women, desire, the body, and enlightenment itself, I became free to celebrate what remains timeless and all-embracing in them.

There are, I have come to believe, three main ways in which the Dhammapada's teachings are timeless and relevant to all seekers on all paths:

The first way is in the Buddha's unwavering awareness of suffering and evil. Karen Armstrong writes in her wonderful biography of the Buddha:

> There is a creeping new orthodoxy in modern society that is some-
> times called "positive thinking." At its worst, this habit of optimism
> allows us to bury our heads in the sand, deny the ubiquity of pain in
> ourselves and others, and to immure ourselves in a state of deliber-
> ate heartlessness to ensure our emotional survival. The Buddha would
> have had little time for this. In his view, the spiritual life cannot begin
> until people allow themselves to be invaded by the reality of suffering,
> realize how fully it permeates our whole experience, and feel the
> pain of all other beings, even those whom we do not find congenial.

The banal pseudo-cheerfulness of much of New Age spirituality cannot help us in a time like ours when we are going to have to, without illusion or false consolation, face up to everything we are doing to each other and to nature if we are to have a chance of survival.

The second area in which the teachings of the Dhammapada are timelessly relevant are in the Buddha's constant insistence on the necessity of training and "guarding" the mind. No other person in human history has analyzed with such calm ruthlessness how our ongoing reality mirrors the inner state of our thoughts and intentions. The unexamined life held no charm whatsoever for the Buddha. He knew how savage and destructive its thoughtlessness could be, and he knew how hard it is to keep the mind constantly in the stream of compassion and insight, and so he stressed the necessity for meditation and intense dedication to spiritual practice. This greatest of all pragmatists makes it clear to all seekers that on the path to self-realization no magical solutions or quick fixes will work. What will work in the end is work. As the Buddha said on his deathbed, refusing one last time to flatter or make any false promises,

"Work out your own salvation with diligence." As it is said in the Dhammapada: "By one's self evil is left undone; by one's self one is puri-fied.... Be not thoughtless, watch your thoughts! Draw yourself out of the evil way, like an elephant sunk in mud."

The third timeless aspect of the Dhammapada's teachings lies, I believe, in the Buddha's championship of compassion, not simply as the deepest and noblest of all enlightened virtues but as an active transform-ing force in the world. The core of his teachings can be found in the soar-ing words of the first section, "The Twin Verses":

"She abused me, he beat me, she defeated me, he robbed me." In those who harbor such thoughts, hatred will never cease. "She abused me, he beat me, she defeated me, he robbed me." In those who do not harbor such thoughts, hatred will cease. For never does hatred cease by hatred at any time. Hatred ceases by love. This is an eternal law.

This is perhaps the essential teaching of all the great mystic liberators of humanity—of the Buddha as well as of Jesus and Muhammad. As our world plunges into greater and greater violence and risks the total anni-hilation of human life and nature, the necessity to know the unifying wisdom of love and to live its force in every thought, gesture, vote, and spiritual, political, and economic action becomes ever more absolute.

In the Dhammapada, the Buddha tells us, "Enlightened ones are solid like the earth that endures, steadfast like a well-set column of stone, clear as a lake where all the mud has settled." Without such solidity, endurance, steadfastness, and clarity—fed by springs of transcendent insight and immanent compassion and sustained by spiritual discipline—we are all at the mercy of the hurricane of history, victims of karma and not loving masters of it in and under the Divine.

In one of the most poignant stories in the Pali Canon, a king in a state of terrible depression drove one day through a park full of tall trop-ical trees. The king got out of his carriage and walked among the roots, many of which were as tall as he was. "They were quiet; no discordant voices disturbed their peace." Looking at these magnificent ancient trees, the king was reminded at once of the grandeur and peacefulness of the Buddha. At once, he went back to his chariot and drove immediately to where the Buddha was staying.

In the torment and confusion of our time, the "tall trees and spacious roots" of the Buddha's teachings in the Dhammapada still radiate their empowering peace. To all those who come to them with an open mind and heart, they offer not only what Karen Armstrong calls "a haven of peace in a violent world of clamorous egotism" but also enduring images and proofs of serenity, dignity, and wisdom that can withstand and transcend anything.

> We live happily indeed when we are not hating those who hate us! Among those who hate us let us dwell free from hatred!... We live happily indeed when we are free from greed among the greedy! Among those who are greedy let us dwell free from greed! We live happily indeed when we call nothing our own! We shall be like the bright gods, feeding on happiness!

Buddha and the Dhammapada ☐

Jack Maguire

One of the most beloved and accessible texts in Buddhism, the Dhamma-pada was first put into writing during the period from approximately 50 B.C.E. to 50 C.E., when the earliest recorded body of Buddhist scriptures, the Pali Canon, was created. Pali, closely related to Sanskrit, is the liturgical language of Theravada, the oldest of Buddhism's three major divisions, commonly called vehicles. Today, Theravada prevails in Sri Lanka, Myanmar, Thailand, and other portions of Southeast Asia.

Because of our historically closer relationships with China, Japan, Vietnam, and Tibet, we in the United States and Canada are more familiar with the other two vehicles, Mahayana (the primary vehicle in the first three Asian nations) and Vajrayana, also known as Tibetan Buddhism. Both of these vehicles use Sanskrit as a liturgical language, so we are more accustomed to Sanskrit words in Buddhist literature than their Pali equivalents. Certain Sanskrit words like dharma, karma, and nirvana have even been adopted into the English language. Because of this situation, some common or significant Sanskrit words appear throughout this book, but their Pali equivalents are often provided first to reflect the language of the source.

The Dhammapada occasionally alludes to concepts or practices that belong distinctly to the Theravada vehicle, but the text as a whole is revered in all three vehicles. A comparatively small work of only 422 verses, the Dhammapada forms part of the *Khuddaka Nikaya* ("Short Collection") found in the Pali Canon's *Sutta Pitaka* ("Basket of Writings"). Among the Pali Canon's three basic divisions, the *Sutta Pitaka* is believed to contain the actual discourses of the historical Buddha.

The Pali word *dhamma* (Skt. *dharma*) means "law" in the sense of universal truth, and it is also used in a specific sense to refer to the Buddha's teachings, which Buddhists believe reflect this law. *Pada*, both a Pali and a Sanskrit term, literally means "footstep" or "track" as well as "word" or "verse." Thus the title *Dhammapada* might be translated generally as "Way of the Law" or more precisely as "Path of the Buddha's Teachings."

The word *buddha*, another term common to Pali and Sanskrit, means "the awakened one." It was—and is—a title bestowed upon the great religious teacher Siddhatta Gotama (whose name is more commonly seen in its Sanskrit form, Siddhartha Gautama), founder of the religion that now claims an estimated four hundred million adherents around the world.

Born in 566 B.C.E. into the ruling clan of a city-state in what we now call southern Nepal, the young Siddhartha forsook his wealth, privilege, and family to live as an itinerant monk, seeking an explanation for humanity's suffering as well as a way to end it. During a long night of intense meditation, he became enlightened and realized what came to be known as the Four Noble Truths: There is suffering in the world; suffering has a cause; suffering has an end; and a path exists to end suffering. He went on to teach throughout northeastern India for the next forty-five years, gaining many disciples and widespread respect before his death at the age of eighty in 486 B.C.E. Among other things, he taught that all human beings are capable of evolving into buddhas or, in other words, of "waking up" to full consciousness of their oneness with other beings and the universe. This realization involves a dropping away of the illusion of "self" as a separate entity. Because we are interconnected with everyone and everything else, it is all the more important to be wise and compassionate in every thought, word, and deed.

What the Dhammapada Is About

The Dhammapada doesn't encapsulate the Buddha's teachings in any comprehensive or essential manner. In fact, no single written work in Buddhism does. Buddhism is not a "religion of the book," like Judaism, Christianity, or Islam, all of which are based on a primary body of scriptures. Instead, Buddhism is a religion of individual practice and enlightenment, aided by direction from a living teacher and, to a lesser degree, personal study of Buddhist texts, which point to the truth without transcribing it directly. The virtue of the Dhammapada is that it beautifully, concisely, and viscerally gives the reader a sense of the route a person travels as he or she advances toward realization of his or her inherent perfection.

Far from being a random assemblage of statements and images, the Dhammapada is a carefully constructed work imbued with both spiritual and literary values. Each new topic unfolds in its proper sequence and rhythm, according to what the reader has already absorbed and what remains to be presented. The text begins by describing the fundamental role of mental conditioning in making us who we are. It then paints contrasting portraits of three types or levels of existence: the fool, the wise one, and the enlightened one. It goes on to address specific aspects of experience, conduct, and belief that characterize an individual's transformation from one of these modes of being to another.

The strikingly unified composition and impassioned moral tone of the Dhammapada strongly suggest that it is indeed the product of a single, highly skilled author. Given the power, vigor, and integrity of the oral tradition in Buddhism for centuries after the Buddha's death, it is not difficult to accept the proposal that the Dhammapada consists mostly if not entirely of his actual words. Many of its linguistic devices—for example, repetition, parallelism, alliteration, and well-crafted shifts in meter—lend themselves to easy memorization and faithful oral transmission.

The Dhammapada doesn't cover many pages, but it invites the mind and heart to savor it over a long period, even an entire lifetime. In this respect it is at once a perpetually revealing map and an eternally resonant message.

Selections from the Dhammapada

Note: In the sample verses from the Dhammapada offered here, each verse is numbered first according to its order in the chapter and second according to its order in the work as a whole.

1 The title "Twin Verses" refers to the structure of the chapter, which consists of ten pairs of statements. Each pair phrases the same basic truth, first from a negative point of view, then from a positive one, to illustrate the alternatives each individual faces. This incantatory rhetorical device is common in ancient Indian philosophy.

2 This belief supports Buddhism's emphasis on mental training, including the disciplines of right understanding, right thought, right mindfulness, and right meditation, four parts of the Noble Eightfold Path revealed to the Buddha during his enlightenment experience.

3 The Pali word *dhamma* (Skt. *dharma*), here "eternal law," is also translated as "the truth" or "the way" in a universal sense; or it may refer to the eternal teaching transmitted by the Buddha (in this case, the word is usually capitalized).

4 Mara ("destroyer, death-causer") is an evil tempter, a supernatural being carried over from Hindu to Buddhist cosmology. He appeared mentally to the Buddha during his enlightenment and tried to thwart it. Mara represents bondage to the phenomenal world of pleasure and pain. He is the "death-causer" because it is only due to this bondage that one experiences death. The opposite of the phenomenal cycle of birth, death, and rebirth is nirvana.

☐ The Twin Verses[1]

1 (1) All that we are is the result of what we have thought.[2] It is founded on our thoughts. It is made up of our thoughts. If one speaks or acts with an evil thought, pain follows one, as the wheel follows the foot of the ox that draws the wagon.

2 (2) All that we are is the result of what we have thought. It is founded on our thoughts. It is made up of our thoughts. If one speaks or acts with a pure thought, happiness follows one, like a shadow that never leaves.

3 (3) "She abused me, he beat me, she defeated me, he robbed me": In those who harbor such thoughts, hatred will never cease.

4 (4) "She abused me, he beat me, she defeated me, he robbed me": In those who do not harbor such thoughts, hatred will cease.

5 (5) For never does hatred cease by hatred at any time. Hatred ceases by love. This is an eternal law.[3]

6 (6) Everyone in the world does not know that we must all come to end here; but those who do know, their quarrels cease at once.

7 (7) One who lives looking for pleasures only—uncontrolled sensually, immoderate in diet, idle, and weak—this one Mara[4] will surely overthrow, as the wind blows down a feeble tree.

8 (8) One who does not live looking for pleasures only—well-controlled sensually, moderate in diet, diligent, and strong—this one Mara will surely not overthrow, any more than the wind blows down a mountain of stone.

5 A saffron (golden yellow) robe is worn by a Buddhist monk. This color is most commonly associated with monastics of the Theravada vehicle.

6 The next world refers to the next lifetime, when one may be reborn into one of the five "worlds" or realms of being: demons in various hells, hungry ghosts, animals, human beings, and gods in various heavens. Some schools of Buddhism speak of six realms, adding another realm of demons or demigods.

9 (9) One who wishes to don the saffron robe[5] while still impure, intemperate, and untruthful is unworthy to do so.

10 (10) One who has cleansed the mind and is endowed with temperance and truthfulness is indeed worthy to wear the saffron robe.

11 (11) One who imagines the real as false and sees falsehood as reality never arrives at truth but follows vain desires.

12 (12) One who knows reality as real and falsehood as false arrives at truth and follows worthy aspirations.

13 (13) As rain breaks through a poorly thatched house, lust breaks through an unvigilant mind.

14 (14) As rain does not break through a skillfully thatched house, lust does not break through a vigilant mind.

15 (15) Evildoers mourn in this world and mourn in the next one.[6] They mourn in both. They mourn and grieve when they see the filthiness of their own deeds.

16 (16) Virtuous ones delight in this world and delight in the next one. They delight in both. They delight and rejoice when they see the purity of their own deeds.

17 (17) Evildoers suffer in this world and in the next. They suffer in both. They suffer when they think of the evil they have done. They suffer even more when they continue on the evil path.

18 (18) Virtuous ones are happy in this world and in the next. They are happy when they think of the good they have done. They are even happier when they continue on the good path.

19 (19) Thoughtless ones, even if they can recite many sacred verses but do not follow them, have no claim to a religious life, but are like cowherders counting the cows of others.

7 | The law: *dhamma*. See n. 3 above.

❖ | "When receiving the teachings, it is important to have the correct attitude. It is not practicing the Dharma properly to listen with the intention of gaining material advantage or reputation. Neither should our goal be higher rebirth in the next life, nor should we be wishing only for our own liberation from *samsara*. These are all attitudes we should reject. Instead, let us listen to the teachings with the determined wish to attain the state of omniscience for the sake of all beings."

—His Holiness the Dalai Lama

20 (20) Thoughtful ones, even if they can recite only a few verses but do follow the law[7] and, forsaking lust, hatred, and delusion, possess true knowledge and peace of mind—they, clinging to nothing in this world or the next, have indeed a claim to a religious life.

In Tibetan Buddhism, Vajrapani, protector of the Dharma, represents the spiritual battle against the forces of lust, hatred, and delusion.

Painting by Madhu and Sangita Chitrakar

1 A fletcher is one who makes arrows. Some translations say "archer," indicating the person who actually shoots arrows (and, therefore, can be said to make arrows rest "straight" against the bow so they will fly "straight" to their target). The former translation better reflects the Buddha's teaching in this chapter that we must be the makers of our own minds.

2 Mara: see "The Twin Verses," n. 4.

3 The expression "hidden away in the body" refers to the mind's tendency to identify itself in terms of the physical body, as if it were some elusive ghost lurking within. The Buddha bids us not to have such a narrow sense of self (or mind), but rather to realize that self is one with everything else in the universe. Here, the notion is to tame the mind out of its problematic tendency to act selfishly on its own—"hiding" or "traveling far."

4 The true law: *dhamma*. See "The Twin Verses," n. 3.

5 The phrase "renounced the notions of merit and demerit" (or, as other translators say, "renounced good and evil") refers to the Buddha's teaching that one should not think in terms of dualistic opposites, which tend to be oversimplistic and separatist. Buddhism doesn't deny that one can *perceive* a certain situation as being either positive or negative, but one should recognize this as a perception, not a reality in itself. In addition, one should not be intent upon accruing merit for self-gain.

☐ The Mind

1 (33) As fletchers[1] make straight their arrows, wise ones make straight their trembling, unsteady minds, which are difficult to guard, difficult to hold back.

2 (34) Like a fish taken from the water and thrown on the dry ground, our mind quivers all over in its effort to escape the dominion of Mara.[2]

3 (35) It is good to tame the mind, which is flighty and difficult to restrain, rushing wherever it will. A tamed mind brings happiness.

4 (36) Let wise ones monitor the mind, which is subtle, difficult to perceive, and restless. A mind well monitored brings happiness.

5 (37) Those who bridle their mind, which, being insubstantial, would travel far on its own, hidden away in the body,[3] are free from the bonds of Mara.

6 (38) If one's mind is unsteady, if one does not know the true law,[4] one's wisdom will never be perfect.

7 (39) If one's mind is free from lust and unperplexed, if one has renounced the notions of merit and demerit,[5] if one remains awake and watchful, then one never has to fear.

8 (40) Knowing that one's body is fragile like a clay pot, and making one's mind firm like a fortress, one should attack Mara with the weapon of wisdom. One should then never falter in watching the conquered Mara.

❖ "Meditation provides a way for us to train in the middle way—in staying right on the spot. We are encouraged not to judge whatever arises in our mind; in fact, we are encouraged not to even grasp whatever arises in our mind. What we usually call good or bad we simply acknowledge as thinking, without all the usual drama that goes along with right and wrong. We are instructed to let the thoughts come and go as if touching a bubble with a feather."

—Pema Chödrön

9 (41) Before long—alas!—the body will lie on the ground, bereft of consciousness and despised, like a useless rotten log.

10 (42) Whatever a hater may do to another hater, or an enemy to an enemy, one's own mind wrongly directed will do to one even greater harm.

11 (43) Neither a mother, nor a father, nor any other relative will do to one as great a service as one's own well-directed mind.

1 Thomas Cleary in his translation of the Dhammapada remarks: "The title of this chapter stands for things of the world, which we may heedlessly pursue as vanities even as time and death stalk us, or we may mindfully use constructively to beautify the world if we realize their value."

2 In Buddhist mythology, derived from Hindu mythology, Yama is the ruler of death and the various hellish realms. For an explanation of the five (or, in some schools, six) "realms of being" in Buddhism, see "The Twin Verses," n. 6.

3 Path of the law: *dhammapada.*

4 The image of the garland as an "interweaving of things" is a popular one in Buddhism. One of the most beloved Mahayana scriptures is the *Flower Garland Sutra* or *Avatamsaka Sutra,* which teaches that the Buddha, mind, all sentient beings, and the universe are one and the same.

5 The phrase "earnest disciple" is translated by Juan Mascaró as "wise student," meaning "student" in the Buddhist sense: one who follows the Buddha as teacher.

6 Mara: see "The Twin Verses," n. 4. For a comparable allusion to Mara, see "The Way," verse 2 (and see n. 4).

7 The fifth-century Theravada commentator Buddhaghosha recorded a famous mythological story that he attributed to the Buddha, and upon which this verse is based. It's worth summarizing here as an example of many similar commentaries on Dhammapada verses:

> In one of the myriad Buddhist heavens there lived a god called Garland-weaver who had one thousand wives. One of these wives was on a high bough of a tree picking flowers to adorn her husband when she got distracted by the pleasure of the act. She fell to Earth, where she was born into a wealthy family. After

☐ Flowers[1]

1 (44) Who shall overcome this world, and the world of Yama,[2] and the world of the gods? Who shall find the well-taught path of the law,[3] even as a clever garland weaver picks out the right flower?[4]

2 (45) The earnest disciple[5] shall overcome this world, the world of Yama, and the world of the gods. The earnest disciple shall find the well-taught path of the law, even as a clever garland weaver picks out the right flower.

3 (46) The one who knows that this body is like froth, as unsubstantial as a mirage, will break the flower-tipped arrow of Mara[6] and never see the king of death.

4 (47) Death carries off a person who is gathering flowers with a distracted mind, just as a flood carries off a sleeping village.

5 (48) Death overpowers a person who is gathering flowers for pleasure before this person can achieve any satisfaction.[7]

6 (49) As the bee collects nectar and flies away without harming the flower, its color, or its scent, so let a wise person go among the people and things of this life.

7 (50) Let not a wise person note the perversities of others, nor what they have done or left undone.

8 (51) Like a beautiful flower without scent are the fair but fruitless words of the one who speaks of virtue but does not act accordingly.

she married, people noticed that she constantly made offerings of garlands, saying, "May these alms bring about my rebirth with my husband." Wrongly assuming she meant her mortal husband, people gave her the name "Husband-honorer."

When Husband-honorer died at an advanced age, she was reborn into the presence of the god Garland-weaver. "We have not seen you since morning," he complained. Husband-honorer told him about her life as a mortal. Describing it as "a mere one hundred years long," she said, "Humans are always reckless, as if they were born to a life of an incalculable number of years, and were never to grow old and die."

To sum up the story, the Buddha recited this verse.

The lotus, a beautiful water lily that grows in the mud, is a symbol in Buddhism for the true, inner perfection of each human being, even though he or she lives in a world of corruption.

9 (52) Like a beautiful flower full of scent are the fair and fruitful words of the one who speaks of virtue and acts accordingly.

10 (53) Even as one may fashion many fine wreaths from a heap of flowers, so should one born to the mortal lot make from it many fine deeds.

11 (54) The scent of flowers does not travel against the wind, nor that of sandalwood, rosebay, or jasmine. But the fragrance of good people travels even against the wind. Thus a good person pervades the universe.

12 (55) Among the scents of sandalwood, rosebay, the blue lotus, and jasmine, the perfume of virtue is the best.

13 (56) Not far from this world travels the scent of rosebay or sandalwood. But the perfume of virtue rises up to the highest gods.

14 (57) The path of those who are virtuous, diligent, and liberated by the true law can never be found by Mara.

15/16 (58/59) Even as a lotus may grow from roadside garbage and spread joy to many traveling souls with its scent, so a true follower of the Buddha shines and brings light to multitudes of blind mortals.

1 The Noble Eightfold Path is cited in the Four Noble Truths (see n. 2 below) revealed during the Buddha's enlightenment. Its eight parts can be described as: right understanding, right thought, right speech, right action, right livelihood, right effort, right mindfulness, and right meditation.

Easwaran notes that Buddhist scriptures offer little discussion of this path, despite its importance. He explains that it was meant to be conveyed orally—i.e., directly—from teacher to student. Also, as this chapter emphasizes, the way can only be "seen" through personal experience.

2 The Four Noble Truths are commonly expressed as: (1) All life is suffering; (2) The cause of suffering is desire; (3) Suffering can be ended; (4) The way to end suffering is the Noble Eightfold Path.

3 The one who sees: that is, a seer, one with "purity of vision" (see verses 5–7).

4 Mara: the evil being who tried to tempt the Buddha during his enlightenment. Among other tricks, he shot the Buddha with passion-tipped arrows to inflame his sensuality as Mara's daughters danced lasciviously before him. Note the different but related arrow symbol in verse 3.

5 The arrow of suffering: an image in Buddhism (especially prevalent in Tibetan Buddhist art) symbolizing any desire to cling or attach that painfully lodges itself in one's existence. The image implies that any source of suffering needs to be removed swiftly, without prior philosophical consideration, spiritual treatment, or any other form of procrastination. In a famous anecdote in the *Cula Malunkaya Sutta,* the

□ The Way

1 (273) The best of paths is the eightfold.[1] The best of truths are the four.[2] The best of mental states is freedom from attachments. The best of human beings is the one who sees.[3]

2 (274) This is the way. There is no other that leads to purity of vision. Go on this way! So shall you confound Mara.[4]

3 (275) If you go on this way, you will make an end of suffering. The way was taught by me after I had understood the removal of the arrow of suffering.[5]

Buddha says, "Suppose a man is wounded by a poisoned arrow and says, 'I will not let this arrow be taken out until I know who shot me, his caste, his family [and so on]....' He would die before he could find out any of these things!"

6 *Tathagatas*: "thus-gone" or "thus-perfected" ones. *Tathagata* is a title referring to the Buddha and, in extension, to any and all enlightened beings.

7 Conditioned things: Pali *samkharas*, phenomena made up of the five conditions or aggregates: matter, sensation, perception, mental formation, and consciousness. The Buddha taught (hence the quotation marks in verse 5) that nothing in the apparently real world exists except as a combination of these aggregates. In other words, nothing has an independent identity of its own.

8 All states: In many translations, the Pali phrase *sabbe dhamma* is translated "all conditioned things" to continue the parallelism of the preceding two verses (a rhetorical device for emphasis). But as Rahula points out, "the word *dhamma* is much wider than *samkhara*. It includes not only the conditioned things..., but also the non-conditioned, the Absolute, Nirvana. There is nothing in the universe or outside, good or bad, conditioned or non-conditioned, relative or absolute, which is not included in this term."

9 Three courses of action: speech, mind, and body. In Buddhist liturgy, these are the three agents that give form to the three poisons of greed, anger, and ignorance. For example, in the Japanese Zen *fusatsu* (renewal of vows) ceremony, monastics declare atonement for all evil committed "because of greed, anger, and ignorance born of my body, mouth, and thought."

10 Meditation: Pali *bhavana,* which can also refer to a specific meditation program rather than simply to meditation. Hence, some translations read "meditative practices" or even "spiritual yoga" (in Sanskrit, *yoga* means "discipline" or "practice").

4 (276) You yourself must make the effort. The *tathagatas*[6] are only teachers. Meditators who enter the way are freed from the bondage of Mara.

5 (277) "All conditioned things[7] are impermanent." The one who knows and perceives this fact ceases to be miserable. This is the way to purity of vision.

6 (278) "All conditioned things are involved in suffering." The one who knows and perceives that fact ceases to be miserable. This is the way to purity of vision.

7 (279) "All states are selfless and unreal."[8] The one who knows and perceives that fact ceases to be miserable. This is the way to purity of vision.

8 (280) One who does not arise when it is time to arise, who is full of sloth though vital and strong, who is weak in will and thought— that lazy and idle one will never find the way to wisdom.

9 (281) Watching speech and carefully restraining the mind, let one never commit any wrong with the body. Let one but keep these three courses of action[9] clear, and one will achieve the way taught by the wise.

10 (282) Through meditation,[10] wisdom is won. Through lack of meditation, wisdom is lost. Let one who knows this two-way path of win and loss behave so that wisdom may be gained.

11 On one level, this statement can refer to doing a complete job in ridding oneself of clinging desires, rather than just a partial one. Thomas Cleary points out another interpretation according to traditional Buddhist symbolism: "The classic Zen master Baizhang said, 'The forest symbolizes mind, the tree symbolizes the body. Fear is aroused because of talk about the forest, so it is said, 'Chop the forest, not the tree.' This underscores the point that Buddhist abstinence and renunciation do not mean torturing the body but rather clearing the mind."

12 Free: You will attain enlightenment.

13 This verse was originally addressed only to monks, and so it represented a direct plea for celibacy. However, as applied to laypeople today, it is not meant to imply that men should give up or separate themselves from women (or vice versa). Instead, the issue is not harboring *lust* for them. Throughout the Dhammapada, one is warned against "attachment" of this kind, meaning any passion-based desire to cling, because it inevitably breeds suffering. For a similar warning, see verse 15. As distinct from lust, which implies an individual self and a separate other (attacher-attachee), true love involves selflessly, compassionately, and wisely becoming one with the beloved and everything else one encounters in the universe.

14 Uprooting a lotus in autumn: that is, weeding out a plant that is dead or dying by autumn.

15 The Happy One: Pali *Sugata,* one of the Buddha's epithets. The word connotes both joy and blessedness.

16 Nirvana: Pali *nibbana,* literally "extinction"; variously interpreted as the end of suffering; release from the cycle of birth and death into an entirely different, higher mode of being; or enlightenment. It should not be confused with the word "death" in the rest of this chapter, which is used to refer to the end of a physical lifetime.

17 The daydreaming fool of this verse is obviously obsessed with material comfort in the world of time and events—a preoccupation that keeps him or her from pursuing the way in this lifetime before it is too late. In India, the monsoon season is late summer.

18 Children are no help…: that is, no help in finding the way.

11 (283) Cut down the whole forest, not one tree only![11] Danger comes out of the forest. When you have cut down the forest and its undergrowth, then you will be free![12]

12 (284) So long as a man's lust for a woman is not overcome, so long is his mind in bondage, as the suckling calf is bound to its nursing mother.[13]

13 (285) Cut out the love of self, like uprooting a lotus in autumn with your hand![14] Cherish the road of peace. The Happy One[15] has shown the way to nirvana.[16]

14 (286) "Here I shall dwell during the monsoon season, here in winter, here in early summer."[17] Thus the fool fancies and does not think of death.

15 (287) Death comes and carries off the one whose mind is wholly caught up in children and possessions, as a flood carries off a sleeping village.

16 (288) Children are no help, nor a parent, nor other relations.[18] There is no help from kinfolk for one whom Death has seized.

17 (289) One who is wise and good and knows the meaning of what is said here should quickly clear the way to nirvana.

3 ■ Jesus

The mystical Jesus as imagined in an early mosaic

Walking with Jesus □

It has always seemed to me far more than a vivid coincidence that in 1945 should occur both the first lethal explosions of the nuclear bomb at Hiroshima and Nagasaki, and the discovery in a small desert cave near Nag Hammadi, in upper Egypt, of a lost gospel, now known as the Gospel of Thomas. It is as if, at the very moment when humanity was brought face to face with its most extreme capacities for horror, evil, and destruction, so also, in Jesus' astonishing, incandescent vision of the Kingdom in the Gospel of Thomas, humanity was shown what it could still achieve if only it woke up and realized the splendor of its divine secret identity. The almost sixty years since then have only emphasized more and more intensely the challenge implicit in this synchronicity; are we, as a race, going to continue pursuing the self-destructive vision that is now plunging the world into war, ruining the environment, and creating for everyone an increasingly degraded and ugly planet, or are we going to take up the ecstatic challenge of Jesus in the Gospel of Thomas to see that the Kingdom already exists in and around us and is only waiting for our transformed insight and for the action that flows from it to break into flame and change everything?

The Gospel of Thomas is more than the most exciting archaeological find of the last century, more even than another gospel to add to the four canonical ones. It is far more than another Gnostic text, or one that carries on the tradition of Jewish wisdom sayings, or, as some have also claimed, a cross between the two. These are scholarly descriptions and distinctions, fascinating and helpful in their way, but they do not begin to describe the extraordinary importance of the Gospel of Thomas, or to show how it can be used today by all sincere seekers to awaken their divine identity and to focus its powers on a radical transformation of the world.

The Gospel of Thomas really is, I believe, the clearest guide we have to the vision of the world's supreme mystical revolutionary, the teacher known as Jesus. To those who learn to unpack its sometimes cryptic sayings, the Gospel of Thomas offers a naked and dazzlingly subversive representation of Jesus' defining and most radical discovery: that the living Kingdom of God burns in us and surrounds us in the glory at all moments, and that a vast and passionate love-consciousness—what you might call "Kingdom-consciousness"—can help birth it into reality. This discovery is the spiritual equivalent of Albert Einstein's and J. Robert Oppenheimer's uncovering of the potential of nuclear fission; it makes available to all humanity a wholly new level of sacred power. By fusing together a vision of God's divine world with a knowledge of how this divine world could emerge into and transfigure the human one, the Gospel of Thomas makes clear that Jesus discovered the alchemical secret of transformation that could have permanently altered world history, had it been implemented with the passion and on the scale that Jesus knew was possible. Its betrayal by the churches erected in Jesus' name has been a disaster, one major reason for our contemporary catastrophe.

Unlike the Buddha, or Krishna, or any of the Eastern sages whose wisdom of transcendent knowledge left fundamentally intact the status quo of a world often characterized as illusory, the Jesus we see in the Gospel of Thomas saw and knew this world as the constant epiphany of the divine Kingdom and knew too that a wholly new world could be created by human beings, once they had allowed themselves to be transformed and empowered as he was, by divine wisdom, ecstasy, and energy. What Jesus woke up to and proceeded to enact with the fiercest imaginable intensity was this new life of "Kingdom-consciousness," not as a savior and not as a guru claiming unique status and truth—the Gospel of Thomas makes this very clear—but as a sign of what is possible for all human beings who dare to awaken to the potential splendor of their inner truth and the responsibilities for total transformation of the world that it then inspires within them.

Jesus' full revolutionary vision in all its outrageousness, grandeur, and radical passion is to be discovered in a close reading of the Gospel of Thomas. The greatest of the sayings are like the equations of physicists Werner Heisenberg or Niels Bohr—complex but intensely lucid expositions in mystical and yogic terms of the laws and potential of a new reality, an endlessly dynamic and fecund reality released from our illusory perceptions and their sterile hunger for separation, division, and stasis.

What I have discovered on my own journey into an increasingly challenging understanding of "Kingdom-consciousness" is that as I continue to uncover and develop in my own depths the "fire" that Jesus speaks of in the Gospel of Thomas, reading the sayings by the brilliant light of this "fire" becomes even more astonishing. The sayings expand in radiance, significance, and reach as I expand my own awareness of divinity and of the powers available to all those who dare to risk transformation.

What I want to offer here is a linked reading of seven of the sayings that have most inspired me. Through this linked reading, I hope to open up to seekers everywhere the full power, as far as I understand it now, of what Jesus is trying to communicate through the Gospel of Thomas, not just to Christians but to the whole of humanity.

Let us begin with saying 2:

Jesus said: The seeker should not stop until he finds. When he does find, he will be disturbed. After having been disturbed, he will be astonished. Then he will reign over everything.

This saying suggests that the Jesus who is speaking in the Gospel of Thomas is not presenting himself as a Messiah with a unique realization and a unique status of mediator. This Jesus—for me, the authentic Jesus—is, like the Buddha, a human being who was awakened to the full glory of his inner divinity and so knows the secret of every human being and hungers to reveal it to change the world. The life to which this Jesus is inviting everyone is not one of endless seeking, but one of finding—finding the truth and power of human divinity by risking everything to uncover them.

From his own harrowing experience, Jesus knows that finding cannot be without suffering; to find out the truth and power of your inner divinity is to be "disturbed": disturbed by the gap between your human shadow and its dark games, and the abyss of light within; by the price that any authentic transformation cannot help but demand; by the grandeur you are beginning to glimpse of your real royal nature with all its burden of responsibility and solitude. Jesus knows too, however, that if you risk this disturbance and surrender to the unfolding of your divine nature, extraordinary visions will be awoken in you—visions that will astound you and drag you into what the Sufi mystics call the "king-dom of bewilderment" that "placeless place" where everything you have imagined to be true about yourself or about humanity is reduced to rubble by the splendor of what you discover. And from this increas-ingly astonishing self-discovery, tremendous powers to influence and transform reality will be born in you. Just as unprecedented energy is unleashed by the splitting of an atom, so through the "splitting" of human identity to reveal the divine identity within it, a huge new trans-forming power is born, a ruling power, the power that great saints and sages have displayed through gifts of healing, miracles, and undaunted stamina of sacred passion and sacrifice. The seeker that becomes a finder and ruler makes a leap in evolutionary development from a human being, unconscious of the Divine hidden within him or her, to an empowered divine human being, capable in and under the Divine of flooding reality with the glory of the Kingdom. To reveal this secret, live it out, and release it in all its radical power, to make "finders" and rulers of us all, is why the Jesus of the Gospel of Thomas lived and preached and died.

This empowering vision of saying 2 leads naturally, as in the text itself, to the challenge of saying 3.

> Jesus said: If your leaders say to you "Look! The Kingdom is in the sky!" Then the birds will be there before you are. If they say that the Kingdom is in the sea, then the fish will be there before you are.

Rather the Kingdom is within you and it is outside of you. When you understand yourselves you will be understood.... If you do not know yourselves, then you exist in poverty and you are that poverty.

The radicalism of this saying should not be underestimated; Jesus is, consciously and with the most subversive imaginable scorn, mocking *all* versions of the spiritual journey that place the ultimate experience beyond this world, in some transcendent "otherwhere." All the patriarchal religions and mystical transmission systems—including those conceived in Jesus' honor—subtly devalue the immanent in favor of the transcendent. This addiction to transcendence with its rhetoric of "the world as an illusion" keeps intact the status quo in all its misery, horror, and injustice.

In saying 3, Jesus ridicules and exposes this evasion of the inherent glory of life and of the world and the stifling of revolutionary vision, ardor, and energy that it entails. He knows that if the Divine is located *outside* human experience and the world, then the vast powers that saying 2 celebrates (that enable the realized mystic to "reign over everything") *cannot* flood the real world to transform its awful conditions.

What Jesus' realization had given him was a comprehensive vision of what he calls the Kingdom as both within and outside himself—both "within" himself as divine consciousness, with all its attendant powers, and "without" himself as divine presence in every detail of creation and as divine potential for the transformation of every aspect of world-life into that of the living kingdom of God's love and justice. The history of Christianity, and so of the world, would have been utterly, and majestically, different had Jesus' crucial fusion of "inner" self-knowledge with "outer" inspired action in every arena been acknowledged in its full demand. Jesus' location of the Kingdom not in "heaven" but in a revolutionary and "earthy" divine awareness—which sees all creation bathed in the glory of the Presence and knows the world potentially transformable into a living fire-mirror of God's wild love for all beings and of God's justice—challenges not only all the churches created in his name but also all of the "transcendentalist" mystical philosophies of the past and future. For

Jesus, these are all too smug, too comfortable in their turning-away from the real human task—that of realizing the Kingdom "within" *and* "without" and then acting with increasingly divinized compassion, knowledge, and power to transform the real world into the world of the Kingdom, not only in "spiritual" but also in cultural, societal, economic, and political ways. For Jesus, aware as he was all-too-piercingly of the scandal of the world's cruelty and pain, not to be pledged to the transfiguration of world-life in every way is to be part of the "poverty" that keeps the world's atrocious games going. "If you do not know yourselves [and do not know the powers or claim the responsibilities that flame from that knowledge],...*then you are that poverty.*"

In saying 8, Jesus makes clear what daring to know the truth of yourself will demand and cost: nothing less than a total commitment to the Divine and a total reversal of the ordinary values of the untransformed world.

> And he said: The man is like a thoughtful fisherman who threw his net into the sea and pulled it out full of little fish. Among all the little fish, that thoughtful fisherman found one fine large fish that would be beneficial to him and, throwing all the little fish back into the sea, he easily chose to keep the large one. Whoever has ears to hear let him hear.

Superficially heard, that saying seems fairly obvious. It seems to be saying that "Kingdom-consciousness" is life's ultimate treasure and all lesser things should be given up for it. Dig deeper and you will see that the saying reveals just what this giving up of lesser things will entail. It is, after all, crazy for a fisherman trying to earn a living to throw back all the "little fish"; it reverses all comfortable laws of commerce or livelihood. And this is precisely Jesus' point—one he makes relentlessly throughout the Gospel of Thomas. If you really want to become a mystical revolutionary, dedicating your life to seeing and enacting "Kingdom-consciousness," you are going to have to surrender all conventional ways of being, acting, or living, and all conventional games of status or power. You are going to have to risk the divine madness that is the true sanity of the fisherman, who so clearly sees and knows the ultimate value of "the large fine fish" that he is willing to throw back all the "little fish" and risk poverty and the contempt of his world to stay true to that divine reality that overturns and potentially transforms all worldly realities. The way of life that Jesus advocates throughout the Gospel of Thomas is in the starkest imaginable contrast to the conservative, prosperity-conscious, family-centered, rule-ridden ethos so often promulgated in his name. For the Jesus of the Gospel of Thomas, only a life of wandering poverty, abandonment to the winds of God, and resolute refusal of the false securities of dogma, authority, or worldly or conventional religious rules of conduct and purity can bring you to the state of utter authenticity and surrender that give birth to the Kingdom in you and make you a revolutionary agent of its birth in reality.

From what I have said, it should now be clear why in saying 10 Jesus announces, "I have thrown fire on the world. Look! I watch it until it blazes." The "fire" that Jesus has thrown—and is constantly throwing on the world—is the fire of a revolutionary transcendent and immanent knowledge and love that menaces all the world's political, social, economic, and religious hierarchies and elite, and all their self-serving justifications for keeping a vicious and unjust set of structures in place. The Jesus of Thomas is not the tender, often ethereal victim of standard Christian legend, or the suffering servant; he is the most fiery-eyed of revolutionaries, a being who knows he has discovered the nuclear secret of a new, potentially all-transforming power of love-in-action, and he is committed to seeing its unleashing upon the world and the transfiguration of the world's laws in its fire. In saying 71, he announces cryptically, "I will destroy this house." Scholars have taken him to mean that either he will bring down the Temple, with all its elite and hierarchy and business policies, through a revelation of a direct egalitarian vision of human divinity, or that he is pledged to destroying the House of Herod that is currently "defiling" the House of David. These are entirely too limiting and local interpretations of the enterprise of Jesus. The Jesus of Thomas is not a peacemaker; he is an incendiary of love, a pyromaniac of divine passion,

announcing the laws of a transformed world and of the enormous strug-
gles, sacrifices, and sufferings, both internal and external, necessary to
engender it. As he proclaims in saying 16, "People think, perhaps, that I
have come to throw peace upon the world. They don't know that I have
come to throw disagreement upon the world, and fire, and sword, and
struggle."

Jesus has far too mordant an understanding of ruthlessness and corruption not to realize that only divine violence can end human violence—
only a sacred violence of abandon to God and commitment to
transformation can dissolve the human violence that keeps the world sunk
in degradation. Not only does Jesus know this, but he faces its necessity
and lives it out in the extremity of his own life (after his very first public
sermon, the Gospel of Matthew tells us, attempts on his life were made).
He is fully aware that his knowledge of the laws of the birth of the Kingdom threaten all previous human accommodations to the way of the
world. Unlike many of the gurus and so-called teachers of our time,
whose vague transcendental waffling further drugs an already comatose
culture and leaves every aspect of the status quo intact, Jesus' vision of
the new way was rooted not only in visionary ecstasy but in an utterly illusionless and ruthless analysis of power in all of its aspects. This is what
made him—and makes him—dangerous, perpetually scandalous, and
what makes the Gospel of Thomas a fiery challenge, not only to less
incendiary versions of his own message, but to all philosophies that do not
propose a complex mystical revolution on every level.

Jesus risked such an almost alienating fervor and uncompromising
urgency of address not merely because he understood that the Kingdom
could not be birthed by any less absolute a passion, but because he knew
too, from the majesty and astonishment of his own experience, that
empowerment on a scale as yet undreamed of awaited any being radical
enough to accept and risk the terms of transformation he was proposing.
Anyone who reads the Gospel of Thomas with an open mind and awakened heart will realize that what Jesus was trying to create was not an

ethical or sociopolitical revolution alone; he was attempting to birth a fully divine human race, a race of beings as radically alive and aware as he was himself. In saying 108, he makes this clear: "Jesus said: He who drinks from my mouth will become like I am, and I will become he. And the hidden things will be revealed to him."

It is in saying 13, however, that the fullest vision of how Jesus wished to empower others is given:

> Jesus asked his disciples: Make a comparison; what am I like? Simon Peter replied: You are like a righteous messenger. Matthew replied: You are like an intelligent lover of wisdom. Thomas replied: Teacher, I cannot possibly say what you are like. Jesus said to Thomas: I am not your teacher; you have drunk from and become intoxicated from the bubbling water that I poured out. Jesus took Thomas and they withdrew. Jesus said three things to him. When Thomas returned to the other disciples, they asked him: What did Jesus tell you? Thomas replied: If I tell you even one of the sayings that he told me, you would pick up stones and throw them at me, and fire would come out of those stones and burn you up.

This is one of the most permanently astonishing of all of the sayings of Thomas, and nothing like it is found in any of the synoptic gospels. What saying 13 makes clear is that what Jesus most wanted was to set others on fire with the same fire with which he himself had been ignited, so that they, like him, could be divinized. Thomas is the one disciple in the saying who does not have a tidy and dead category through which to express his understanding of Jesus. Thomas has become a "finder" and so is bewildered and astonished: "Teacher, I cannot possibly say what you are like." One last block remains to Thomas's true understanding of Jesus and who and what he is—Thomas's own reverence of Jesus as "teacher," a reverence, however beautiful and justified, that acts as a subtle distancing force from the full outrageousness of the truth. That full outrageousness Jesus proceeds with his usual nakedness to uncover: "I am not your teacher, you have drunk from and become intoxicated from the bubbling water that I have poured out." Jesus recognizes that

Thomas has allowed himself not merely to try to follow him, but has risked everything by getting drunk from the "bubbling water" of divine knowledge and divine passion that Jesus has poured out for him, and in so doing, he has become like Jesus himself, one with him and one with his fiery source.

If all the Gospel of Thomas did was relentlessly and sublimely champion the path to our transfiguration and point out its necessity, it would be one of the most important of all religious writings—but it does even more. In saying 22, the Gospel of Thomas gives us a brilliantly concise and precise "map" of the various stages of transformation that have to be unfolded in the seeker for the "secret" to be real in her being and active though all her powers. Like saying 13, saying 22 has no precedent in the synoptic gospels and is, I believe, the single most important document of the spiritual life that Jesus has left us.

> Jesus saw infants being suckled. He said to his disciples: These infants taking milk are like those who enter the Kingdom. His disciples asked him: If we are infants will we enter the Kingdom? Jesus responded: When you make the two into one, and when you make the inside like the outside and the outside like the inside, and the upper like the lower and the lower like the upper, and thus make the male and the female the same, so that the male isn't male and the female isn't female. When you make an eye to replace an eye, and a hand to replace a hand, and a foot to replace a foot, and an image to replace an image, then you will enter the Kingdom.

There are four interlinked truths about saying 22 that I would like to unravel here, for they each illustrate another aspect of Jesus' vision of "Kingdom-consciousness" and, taken together, provide the fullest guideline we have to its implementation and power.

First, we see "Kingdom-consciousness" in the Child, born from a marriage of opposites—of transcendence and immanence, heart and mind, soul and body, masculine and feminine. The freedom and mastery of this "Divine Child consciousness" transcends all known categories, prepares a wholly new birth in every dimension, and brings the seeker into unity with the One in all its aspects and potential.

Second, we see the agency of this transformation in the motherhood of God, the Divine Feminine. This is quite clear from the image of infants sucking at the breast, through which Jesus is trying to make us aware of the importance of the embodied Godhead, the Mother aspect of God, and how important it is to the kind of transformation he wants. Only those who have awoken to the Kingdom within *and* without as the embodied Godhead will be able to view life and creation and all the workings of the universe with the kind of abandon and trust that will allow them to be fed directly by God, with all the powers of vision and action they need. Without a restoration to the Christian mysticism of Jesus' own full celebration of the Divine Feminine, the "Kingdom-consciousness" cannot and will not be born.

The third truth that saying 22 reveals is the order of the transformations that have to be undergone by every seeker if "Kingdom-consciousness" is to be realized. The first recognition—when you make the two into one—describes the first major inner revelation of the divine consciousness, that of the impotence of all dualistic concepts to begin to describe Reality. This is followed by the opening of the heart center (known as the heart-chakra in Hinduism, Sufism, and Buddhism), which dissolves all distinction of inner and outer in a living vision of all things burning in divine light. This in turn leads to the collapse of all previously useful categories of high and low, sacred and profane, through the revelation of Presence in all things, events, actions, and possibilities—what in Hinduism and Buddhism is known as the Tantric revelation of Nirvana as Samsara, of the world of appearance as being essentially one with Absolute Reality and saturated at all moments with divinity. The combination of an experience of all three linked revelations leads to the alchemical fusion within the seeker of masculine and feminine, and so to the mutual transformation of the "masculine" powers of will, order, logic, and strength, by the "feminine" powers of compassion, sensitivity, and reverence for all life. That engenders a new kind of being, the Divine Child or Sacred Androgyne who, like the Divine itself, is beyond category and able to use transformed feminine and masculine powers in whatever combination is called for by the actual situation. Such a being "reigns" over reality in the name of and with some of the actual miraculous powers of the Divine itself. When Jesus says in saying 19 "If you become my disciples and listen to me, these stones will serve you," in saying 24 "There is light within a man of light, and he lights up all of the world," and in saying 106 "When you make the two into one, you will be called sons of men. When you say 'Move, mountain!' it will move," he was not speaking in incandescent poetry; he was describing the actual powers that God gives those who risk becoming divinized, powers that can alter natural law and "burn down the house" of the oppressive power structures of the world.

Fourth and finally, we come in saying 22 to its final cryptic sentences: "When you make an eye to replace an eye, and a hand to replace a hand, and a foot to replace a foot, and an image to replace an image, then you will enter the Kingdom." What these lines describe is nothing less than the physical transformation that mystical union makes possible, the bringing up of ordinary matter into the living truth of the Light. The ultimate sign of the Christ is the victory of the Resurrection, which is the marriage of matter and spirit to create a wholly new and eternal substance. Those mystics who follow Christ into union come to know and taste the glory of the Resurrected Body in their own bodies. The powers available to the human being willing to undertake the full rigor of the Jesus-transformation are limitless. What could not be done to transform this world by a group of seekers who allowed their whole beings—psychological, spiritual, and physical—to become increasingly transfigured by the living light? The greatest of all modern philosophers—Sri Aurobindo—saw that only an "integral" transformation could provide the force and inspiration to change that must occur if humanity is to survive and evolve. Jesus in saying 22 has anticipated Sri Aurobindo's vision and provided the map to its realization.

There may be very little time left to take the adventure into total being that the Gospel of Thomas advocates with such astringent brilliance and precision. In such a terrible age as ours, it is easy to believe that the dark powers, the powers of that "corpse" of the world that the Jesus of Thomas so fiercely denounces, have won already, and there is nothing even the most passionate of us can do to turn around a humanity addicted to violence and destruction.

Despair, however, is the last illusion. The Gospel of Thomas and the Jesus who gave it to us continue to challenge us to dare to become one with the Divine and start living the revolutionary life that streams from union and that can transform all things. This worst of times needs the clearest and most unflinchingly exigent of visions to counteract and transform it; in Jesus' words in the Gospel of Thomas and in his living out of their reality through and beyond death itself into the eternal empowering glory of the Resurrection, we have the permanent sign of the Way, the Truth, and the all-transforming life that, even now, can build here on earth the reality of God's Kingdom.

Title page of the original Coptic Gospel of Thomas

Jesus and the Gospel of Thomas ▢

Stevan Davies

For those interested in Jesus of Nazareth and the origins of Christianity, the Gospel of Thomas is the most important manuscript discovery ever made. Apart from the canonical scriptures and a few scattered sayings, the Gospel of Thomas is our only historically valuable source for the teachings of Jesus. Although it has been available in European languages since the 1950s, it is still subject to intense scrutiny and debate by biblical scholars. The Gospel of Thomas is roughly the same age as the canonical New Testament gospels, but it contains sayings of Jesus that present very different views on religion and on the nature of humanity and salvation, and it thereby raises the question whether the New Testament's version of Jesus' teachings is entirely accurate and complete.

In late 1945, an Egyptian peasant named Mohammed Ali al-Samman Mohammad Khalifa rode his camel to the base of a cliff, hoping to find fertilizer to sell in the nearby village of Nag Hammadi. He found, instead, a large sealed pottery jar buried in the sand. He feared it might contain a genie that would haunt or attack him, and he hoped it might contain a treasure. Gathering his courage, he smashed open the jar and discovered only a collection of twelve old books. Suspecting that they might have value on the antiquities market, he kept the books and eventually sold them for a small sum. The books gradually came into the hands of scholars in Cairo, Europe, and America. Today those books are known as the Nag Hammadi library, a collection that is generally considered to be the most important archaeological discovery of the twentieth century for research into the New Testament and early Christianity. The Nag Hammadi library contains the Gospel of Philip, the Gospel of Truth, the Gospel of the Egyptians, the Secret Book of James, the Secret Book of John, and many other fascinating texts ranging in date from the second through the middle of the fourth centuries A.D. The twelve books contain fifty-two texts altogether, forty of which were previously unknown to scholarship.

Of all the Nag Hammadi texts, by far the most significant is the Gospel of Thomas. Scholars knew of the existence of the Gospel of Thomas before the Nag Hammadi discovery because it was mentioned in the works of Hippolytus, a third-century church father. At the end of the nineteenth century, fragments of the Gospel of Thomas in the Greek language were found in the rich Egyptian archaeological site known as Oxyrhynchus, a discovery that excited great interest among New Testament scholars because the fragments contained sayings of Jesus that were familiar from the New Testament but appeared to have been transcribed from independent oral tradition and therefore were a new source for the teachings of Jesus.

When the full Gospel of Thomas came to light in the Nag Hammadi Library fifty years later, it was excitedly greeted as if it were an old friend. Scholars immediately saw that they now possessed the full version of what they had known before only in fragments. The version of the Gospel of Thomas found at Nag Hammadi, like all the texts in that collection, was written in Coptic, the language of ancient Egypt put into an alphabet derived from (but not entirely identical to) the Greek alphabet. The newly found text was not an original Coptic composition but a translation of a Greek original, the same Greek sayings list that had been found in fragments at Oxyrhynchus.

The Gospel of Thomas contains roughly 150 sayings attributed to Jesus, about half of which are also found in the canonical New Testament gospels of Matthew, Mark, and Luke. It does not contain sayings found also in the Gospel of John. For convenience, scholars have numbered the sayings in a standard sequence, almost always basing the numbers on the occurrence of the phrase "Jesus said." By that method the standard list contains 114 sayings, some of which are two or more sayings combined into one. Thomas contains no sustained narrative at all, although it contains a few narrative elements, for example, "a woman in the crowd said to him" (79), "Jesus saw infants being suckled. He said to his disciples…" (22).

The format of the Gospel of Thomas is little more than a disorganized list. The sayings at the very beginning (sayings 1–3) and end (113) may have been deliberately placed in those locations, but the rest of the sayings, despite the efforts of many scholars over the past half century to find order in them, appear to have been haphazardly put together. To some degree, the Gospel of Thomas begins to repeat sayings toward its end, and several times throughout the text, sayings of the same general sort—short sets of proverbs for example, or parables—appear adjacent to one another. Sometimes adjacent sayings share a word or a motif, but otherwise there's no known order to the list. The Gospel of Thomas is about as primitive a form of text as there can be: a simple list with one thing following another in a manner that is much more reminiscent of oral tradition than of literary construction. It appears most likely that the sayings list we call the Gospel of Thomas was transcribed by a scribe on a particular occasion from the word-of-mouth recitations by some people who were trying to remember what they could of what Jesus reportedly had said.

For most people, the Gospel of Thomas's greatest significance arises from the fact that so many of its sayings are similar to sayings in the canonical gospels. This raises the question whether Thomas is a source for the teachings of Jesus independent of the New Testament gospels, or whether it is dependent on those canonical gospels. If the Gospel of Thomas is independent, its sayings were derived from sources other than the New Testament gospels, most probably from oral rather than written sources. If it is dependent, then its sayings were taken from the New Testament. If it is independent, then the Gospel of Thomas gives us a new source for the teachings of Jesus of Nazareth, our first new source for nearly two thousand years and one second in importance only to the biblical books. On the other hand, if the Gospel of Thomas is dependent on the canonical scriptures, then—while it provides some interesting insight into a very early Christian cult—it offers no new information of significance about Jesus of Nazareth.

Those who argue that Thomas is dependent on the canonical gospels for its sayings point to the fact that, according to the most widely held theory of New Testament origins, the Gospel of Mark was revised by Matthew and Luke as they incorporated it into their own gospels. Accordingly, when a word or phrase appears in Matthew or Luke in a passage they have in common with Mark, but that particular word or phrase does not itself appear in Mark, it generally indicates that Matthew or Luke has changed Mark. Now, if the same word shows up in the equivalent saying in Thomas, some find it reasonable to presume that Thomas found the word in Matthew's or Luke's Gospel and therefore took the saying from that existing gospel. Since this happens on a few occasions, some conclude that Thomas must have used Matthew's and Luke's Gospels as a source.

On the other hand, many scholars argue that there are so few hints of dependence by Thomas on Matthew's or Luke's or Mark's Gospels that the hints that do exist can best be explained by the fact that Christian scribes copied and translated Thomas throughout the centuries before it was hidden at Nag Hammadi. The history of the New Testament manuscript tradition shows that the scribes who copied such manuscripts invariably made mistakes, made what they thought were improvements, copied what they remembered a saying to be rather than what a manuscript in front of them said it was, and so forth. In other words, as scribes copied Thomas they did so in light of their own knowledge of the canonical gospels, and the same would be true for whoever it was who translated the Gospel of Thomas from Greek into Coptic. It is only reasonable to presume that their knowledge of the canonical gospels occasionally led them to change Thomas's sayings as they copied them, and as time went on, sayings in copies of the Gospel of Thomas increasingly came to resemble their New Testament counterparts. Therefore, if on a few occasions Thomas's sayings have words that accord with Matthew's or Luke's version of sayings rather than Mark's version, this does not by any means prove that the Gospel of Thomas is dependent on Matthew's or Luke's Gospels, only that scribes in the chain of copying and translating were familiar with the canonical gospels.

The Gospel of Thomas seems often to contain sayings of Jesus in a less revised state than they are in the canonical gospels. In the words of Professor Helmut Koester of the Harvard Divinity School: "If one considers the form and wording of the individual sayings in comparison with the form in which they are preserved in the New Testament, the Gospel of Thomas almost always appears to have preserved a more original form of the traditional saying or presents versions which are independently based on more original forms. In a few instances where this is not the case, the Coptic translation seems to have been influenced by the translator's knowledge of the New Testament gospels."

Many scholars have noted that Thomas is the most primitive possible form of written tradition, a simple barely organized list, and that to a great extent the sayings in the Gospel of Thomas that do overlap with versions in the canonical gospels show absolutely no sign of having been taken from those gospels. In addition, there is virtually no overlap in the order of the sayings, for virtually none of the sayings in Thomas occur in the same sequence as they do in Matthew or Mark or Luke. All these factors argue for Thomas's independence from the influence of the canonical gospels, as does the fact that the Gospel of Thomas does not contain any reference to the great Christian themes of crucifixion and resurrection, or any reference to Jesus' status as Messiah or Christ, or the stories of him as virgin-born and capable of miraculous actions. One of the most likely reasons for the absence of these concepts is that the Gospel of Thomas was compiled before those Christian themes were fully developed. Significantly, Thomas also lacks the imaginative cosmological speculations typical of later Christian Gnostic texts. It seems to have come into being before those kinds of writings were developed.

The Gospel of Thomas, it now appears, is very likely to be independent of the New Testament's canonical gospels and therefore to be a new source for the teachings of Jesus. Since it is in such a primitive form—the unstructured list—and since it shows no signs of the great themes of Christianity that developed in the early church, and since the forms of the sayings in Thomas are often less developed than they are in the canonical gospels, it stands to reason that Thomas is quite an early text. It may perhaps have been written before 62 A.D., for there is a hint of a date in that period in the Gospel of Thomas itself: saying 12 commends Jesus' brother James to be the leader of the Christian movement after Jesus himself is no longer on earth. James died in the year 62 A.D. It follows that a saying recommending his leadership would probably not have been incorporated into Thomas after that year. Be that as it may, one cannot say for certain when Thomas was written, for, apart from the hint supplied by saying 12, there are no chronological indicators in the text.

There are no clear geographical indicators in the Gospel of Thomas, for it contains no narratives that give us place names. However, we may have one clue in the title of the text itself. In the early days of the Christian movement, different regions claimed different apostles as the founders of their own churches. Mark was said to have founded the church in Egypt, John the church in Greece, Peter the church in Rome, and Thomas the church in Syria. The Acts of Thomas, a late-third-century Syrian pious novel, and the Book of Thomas, which is a fictional fourth-century Syrian dialogue between Thomas and Jesus, testify to a particular Syrian interest in Thomas the apostle. As does the much earlier Gospel of Thomas, those texts refer to "Judas Thomas." Some argue that because of the significance of the apostle Thomas to later Syrian Christianity, the Gospel of Thomas probably comes from Syria. Syria is the northern neighbor of Galilee and had an established Christian community at least by the early 30s A.D. at which time Paul was making his way to Damascus to confront the Christian church there.

Most New Testament scholars find a theory known as the "two-source hypothesis" to be the most convincing way to account for the fact that the Gospels of Matthew, Mark, and Luke are word-for-word identical in the Greek of many passages. The "two-source hypothesis" holds that Matthew and Luke used two texts as principal sources for their own gospels. One of those texts is the narrative we call the Gospel of Mark. The other text is a now lost collection of the sayings of Jesus that German scholarship came to call "the source" or, in German, *Quelle*, or, now quite commonly, just Q. This Q can be reconstructed from the Gospels of Matthew and Luke, for, in the simplest formulation, Q is simply a list of the material that we find in Matthew's and Luke's Gospels that we do not find in Mark's Gospel. Today the two-source hypothesis is so commonly accepted that books are now published discussing Q as though it were a real existing text.

The "two-source hypothesis" was attacked in earlier decades because, for one thing, there was no evidence that Christian communities composed lists of sayings; no list like the hypothetical Q had ever been discovered. But now the discovery of the Gospel of Thomas has confirmed the hypothesis that lists of sayings definitely existed during the earliest times of Christianity.

Today, many scholars of Christian origins will place the reconstructed Q list side by side with the newly discovered Thomas list as the earliest gospels that we have. Q and the Gospel of Thomas are not the same thing. Q, as reconstructed by scholarship, appears to have been somewhat more coherently organized than the Gospel of Thomas and to have begun to take on the form of a narrative of Jesus' life.

Thomas and Q are significantly different in terms of the points of view their contents advocate. The Q list, through its selection of sayings, presents Jesus as a man who taught that the Kingdom of God would come in the very near future. Only a few will be allowed into the Kingdom when it comes, but everyone will see it arrive "like a lightning flash." To be allowed into the Kingdom, one must begin to behave appropriately; one must "do unto others as you would have God do unto you." As you forgive others God will forgive you; as you judge others God will judge you. This combination of future orientation and judgment based on moral behavior has characterized much of Christianity to this day. Like Thomas, however, Q shows no significant interest in the motif of crucifixion and resurrection or salvation through grace and faith.

The sayings in the Gospel of Thomas present a startling contrast to this point of view. Thomas also speaks of the Kingdom of the Father, but here we find that the Kingdom already exists on the earth and has existed since the very beginning of time. When Jesus is asked about the coming of the Kingdom in Thomas, he invariably replies that the Kingdom is here now; it is right in front of your face, even though people usually do not see it. The Gospel of Thomas implies that the Kingdom has always been present, ever since the first days of creation. But its presence is now hidden from almost everyone. One might summarize the Gospel of Thomas as saying: "Find the Kingdom that is right here." Some have compared this perspective to such Eastern philosophies as Zen Buddhism. Few religious texts in the West insist that perfection exists on this earth now, if you can find it. Rather, the Western religions generally place perfection in the heavens and in the future. Thomas's Gospel presents a very different view.

The idea that the Kingdom is already here, but usually undiscovered, leads logically to the idea that a person's greatest accomplishment would be to find the Kingdom. The motif "seek and ye shall find" occurs throughout the Gospel of Thomas. If people are inherently able to find the Kingdom, they nevertheless will need guidance as to how to do it. That is the purpose of the Gospel of Thomas: to give directions toward finding the Kingdom. Those directions, however, are presented in a deliberately obscure fashion. The directions come as riddles, as sayings of Jesus that need to be deciphered in order to be understood. The Gospel of Thomas sets itself up as a model for spiritual endeavor. Just as people should approach its sayings as having deeper hidden meaning that is not immediately apparent, so also should they perceive the world as having deeper hidden meaning.

Thomas conveys a very positive view of human nature. People are capable of discovering hidden truth, both in the world and within themselves.

Indeed, as the Kingdom is already in the world, so it is already inside of people. Accordingly, if you know yourself properly, you know the Kingdom of God. While Thomas has some sayings that point to a moral dimension for human life, its overall approach is structured in terms of self-knowledge and discovery.

Significantly, there is no place in the Gospel of Thomas for the great themes of sin and salvation as they are found in the canonical New Testament. The human problem is not defined as separation from God as a result of one's moral failings or the mythical failings of Adam, nor is the solution presented in terms of faith in the death of Christ for sins, or in reference to the resurrection of Christ. Those themes are absent.

Thomas gives us a whole new kind of first-century Christianity. It has been called a Gnostic Christianity; *gnosis* is the Greek word for knowledge, and the term *gnostic* has *gnosis* at its root. A wide variety of Gnostic Christianities emerged during the second century with increasingly complicated and, to us, bizarre views of the creation and history of the cosmos. Most of the Nag Hammadi collection of texts can be categorized as Christian Gnostic. The Gospel of Thomas, however, is not properly called Gnostic because it completely lacks interest in the history of the cosmos that the later Gnostic texts find so fascinating. Still, Thomas does advocate a point of view that Gnostic Christians also held: that knowledge of the divine and knowledge of oneself are inseparable.

Those who find the Gospel of Thomas interesting often wonder why it is not in the Bible alongside the Gospels of Matthew, Mark, Luke, and John. Unfortunately, there is no good answer to that question because we do not know how the canonical gospels came to be selected in the first place. Around the year 180 A.D., Irenaeus, the bishop of Lyon in what is now France, argued that there should be only the four gospels of the New Testament in the church's official collection. He assumed that his orthodox readers were already well aware that there are four and only four. But how the decision for four and not three and not five came to pass, we do not know. One cannot assume that Thomas was deliberately excluded from the canon of scripture because we have no idea whether those who decided on the canonical four had ever even heard of the Gospel of Thomas. Thomas may have circulated extensively in the Eastern churches, from Syria to Egypt, and yet have remained almost unknown to churches in the West.

The Gospel of Thomas appears at first to be only a sporadic collection of disconnected sayings. But examination of those sayings one by one can lead to a more comprehensive vision of what the compilers of the text intended to communicate. The Gospel must be read carefully, saying by saying, and one must allow the meaning of the whole to build gradually. If one does this successfully, and if one comes to find the right interpretation of the sayings in Thomas, then, the text promises, one "will not taste death."

Selections from the Gospel of Thomas

1 The "hidden-ness" of the sayings has to do with their enigmatic character. The meaning of these sayings is hidden within them as, for example, leaven is hidden in dough (saying 96) or a treasure might be hidden in a field (saying 109). The Gospel of Thomas is optimistic that what is hidden will be revealed (saying 5). These are not sayings that were supposed to be kept secret from other people, though, for roughly half of them are found in Matthew's and Mark's and Luke's Gospels, so it's likely that they were all commonly known and widely circulated.

2 Immortality is said to be the reward of anyone who successfully decodes Thomas's enigmatic sayings. The correct interpretation of the sayings is not the final goal but the means to the goal, the discovery of the Kingdom of Heaven. Thomas's Gospel is an exercise book, a list of riddles for decoding. The secret lies not in the final answers but in the effort to find the answers.

3 This Gospel's Christianity is not based on grace, on salvation given as a gift by God, but on active individual effort. Successful effort will be accompanied by strong emotions, for whatever is to be found will be disturbing and then astonishing. Thomas often uses the motif of "seek and find" (for example, in saying 2), but it is never made clear exactly what it is one is seeking. As did God's Image in Genesis 1:28, human beings will come some day to reign over everything within the worlds that they find within themselves.

☐ Sayings of the Gospel of Thomas

Incipit: These are the hidden sayings that the living Jesus spoke and that Didymus Judas Thomas wrote down.[1]

1 And he said: Whoever finds the correct interpretation of these sayings will never die.[2]

2 Jesus said: The seeker should not stop until he finds. When he does find, he will be disturbed. After having been disturbed, he will be astonished. Then he will reign over everything.[3]

4 Having introduced the principle that the Kingdom is to be sought and found, the Gospel of Thomas parodies two ideas attributed to rival leaders. The Kingdom is not to be found across the sea, and it is not up in the sky. Even today, many people will point to the sky if asked where heaven is to be found. But this saying makes fun of such an idea. The Kingdom is within you, as Luke's Gospel also says (17:20–21). And yet it is also outside. Thomas is a spiritual Gospel, yet it points out to the world of nature and to the realm of all creation instead of pointing only back toward the reader.

5 The idea that self-knowledge is a road to salvation is perhaps as old as philosophy itself. Its most famous occurrence is the inscription "Know Thyself" at the oracle at Delphi. Thomas's statement "the Kingdom is within you and outside of you" places that Gospel in the context of ancient philosophical speculation and affirms the goodness of both human nature and of the nature of the outside world in an unambiguous fashion. Being Sons of the Father is to be like Jesus himself, a status one does not attain anew but that one realizes one has always had. Accordingly, self-discovery is the key to finding the potential wealth buried in people and in the world.

3a Jesus said: If your leaders say to you "Look! The Kingdom is in the sky!" then the birds will be there before you are. If they say that the Kingdom is in the sea, then the fish will be there before you are. Rather, the Kingdom is within you and it is outside of you.[4]

3b When you understand yourselves you will be understood. And you will realize that you are Sons of the living Father. If you do not know yourselves, then you exist in poverty and you are that poverty.[5]

6 The specific symbolism of a "seven-day-old" infant suggests a time before circumcision, which was performed on the eighth day (and according to Thomas, circumcision is a senseless custom [saying 53]). The infant of seven days may also refer to the Image of God, who existed on the seventh day before the second round of creation brought Adam into being. The old man probably represents the ordinary person who has not sought or found the Kingdom. The infant as a model for wisdom can be found in other sayings in this Gospel as well, signifying that people must find a way to return to the beginning of their world and the time of the first creation. Saying 4 implies that the experience of discovery is no respecter of persons. The social categories of youth and age, and being socially first or last—these are irrelevant matters.

7 If what is hidden is the Kingdom, as saying 3 seems to indicate, its location is here in the present world. The Kingdom is everywhere now. In their separate ways, sayings 5 and 3 both deny that one's quest should lead one away from one's present circumstances. This contrasts strikingly with the more familiar early Christian opinion that the Kingdom is an event to be anticipated in the future or that the Kingdom is presently somewhere other than here. It also contrasts with the tendency of mystical speculations to create a complex system of truths that are difficult to comprehend. Thomas declares that it is all very obvious and easy to comprehend, once one has found the key to seeing things in the new way Jesus recommends.

4a Jesus said: The old man will not hesitate to ask a seven-day-old baby about the place of life, and he will live.[6]

4b For there are many who are first who will become last. They will become a single one.

5 Jesus said: Recognize what is right in front of you, and that which is hidden from you will be revealed to you. Nothing hidden will fail to be displayed.[7]

8 Ironically, the vast majority of Christians—in the United States at least—seem to think of Jesus *primarily* as one who came to throw peace upon the world and to bring loving harmony to families. Evidently Jesus disagreed with that assessment. People whose notion of Jesus focuses on his status as "Prince of Peace" seem to be relying exclusively on a phrase found in Isaiah 9:7 but found nowhere in the New Testament.

The final statement "And they will stand up and they will be *alone*" uses the term *monachos*, the Greek word for people who are single or alone; the English word "monk" derives from *monachos*. In Thomas, the word characterizes those who opt out of worldly life to live in the direct presence of the Kingdom of Heaven.

❖ "A number of scholars have developed summaries of this Gospel's theology, but ultimately no summary will be able to capture the interactive and intellectually challenging process of hearing the sayings pronounced by Jesus and finding their interpretation. This attentive reading is, after all, the suggested strategy presented by the Gospel itself."

—Richard Valantasis, The Gospel of Thomas (London and New York: Routledge, 1997), p. 12

16a Jesus said: People think, perhaps, that I have come to throw peace upon the world. They don't know that I have come to throw disagreement upon the world, and fire, and sword, and struggle.

16b [For] there will be five in one house. Three will oppose two. Two will oppose three. The father will oppose his son and the son oppose his father. And they will stand up and they will be alone [*monachos*].**8**

9 Thomas's sayings sometimes are based on the fact that there are two creation stories in Genesis. The first begins at Genesis 1:1 and ends at 2:3. The second begins at 2:4 and continues indefinitely. The first creation is perfect. God declares it "good" seven separate times. The first creation features the origin of light and of the primordial humanity made in the Image of God. The second creation starts as if the first had never taken place and features the creation of man out of dirt and the creation of woman out of the man's rib.

Ancient (and present-day) readers sometimes wondered what happened to the first creation. Such a good creation would not just disappear for no reason. Since the first is never said to have ceased to be, then it must coexist along with the second in a condition of perfection unmarred by any fall subsequent to the primordial seventh day.

From Thomas's perspective, the ultimate goal for human beings is to enter into the condition of the first creation—a condition that continues to exist in reality, although the second creation is what virtually everyone ordinarily perceives. Thomas calls the first hidden creation "the Kingdom of Heaven." The human condition of any person can be that of the original Image of God or that of the Adam from the second creation. Accordingly, those who exist before coming into being are humans in the manner of the Image of God, which existed (Genesis 1:26–27) before humans in the form of Adam came into being (Genesis 2:7). Both continue simultaneously to exist, but the later and inferior form masks the former primordial form.

10 Since the Kingdom of Heaven is here now upon the earth, everything on earth will serve disciples who recognize that fact. We hear in the Genesis story of the first creation that humans will have dominion over all things on earth (Genesis 1:28–30). The very stones serve those who recognize their own true nature and the true nature of the world.

The five trees of paradise may allude to the rivers of the four directions, specified in Genesis 2:11–14 along with the center, Eden, from which the rivers flow (Genesis 2:10). These rivers water the trees of paradise (Genesis 2:9). To come to know the trees of paradise, one must return to the condition of the Beginning.

19a Jesus said: Blessed is one who existed before coming into being.⁹

19b If you become my disciples and listen to me, these stones will serve you.

19c In paradise there are five trees that do not change between summer and winter, and their leaves never fall. Anyone who comes to know them will not die.¹⁰

11 The transformation in perceptions that Thomas's sayings encourage is a very difficult one, and very few people are able to accomplish it. The "seek and find" ideology of Thomas is quite different than the "gift" ideology of the orthodox doctrine of grace. Thomas's sayings encourage individuals to find the Kingdom for themselves, within and outside themselves. Being one of those who are "chosen" therefore gives one the *opportunity* to quest for the Kingdom. It cannot be the case that some few people are "chosen" to receive the Kingdom as a gift.

12 The disciples again take the wrong approach. Their question, which appears to be nonsense, presupposes the orthodox view of Christianity: that Jesus Himself is the be-all and end-all of the Christian faith. Accordingly, finding the place where Jesus is, is what any Christian should do. Rather than find all the world, the orthodox view expressed here in the disciples' question is that finding the one place Jesus is will suffice. Jesus' response encourages breadth of inquiry. Just as saying 3 located the Kingdom within and outside of people, so this saying locates light inside and outside. Individuals' efforts are required. The man of light can illuminate the world or not. The saying assumes the logical possibility that a man of light can be darkness, and therefore his illumination of the world is not automatic and innate.

In order to see the world as the Kingdom of God, one must illuminate the world in a Kingdom-like manner. Therefore, self-transformation must come first. One restores oneself as the Image of God, as saying 22 urges, and at the Beginning, as saying 18 requires. Then one can illuminate the world outside as God's Kingdom in accordance with saying 24. One will then radiate out from within oneself the light of creation's first day, the supernal light that came before the creation of sun and stars.

23 Jesus said: I will choose one of you out of
a thousand and two of you out of ten thousand.
They will stand up and they will be alone.[11]

24 His disciples said to him: Show us the place you
are, for it is essential for us to seek it. He responded:
He who has ears let him hear. There is light within
a man of light, and he lights up all of the world.
If he is not alight there is darkness.[12]

13 The first record of the admonition to "love your neighbor as yourself" occurs in Leviticus 19:18. There its context is negative, focusing on what one should not do: "You should not take vengeance or bear a grudge against any of your people but you should love your neighbor as yourself." Here in the Gospel of Thomas the context is positive: "protect him."

14 This saying concludes with a proverb, common sense expressed cleverly with meaning that shifts depending on the context within which it is spoken. In the present context of saying 24, it admonishes a person of light to begin to shine forth radiance into the world before setting out to show others the way to do so. In the context of saying 25, one can understand it to urge people to prepare to protect their brothers by first making sure that they are strong enough to do so.

❖ "As a gospel of wisdom, the Gospel of Thomas proclaims a distinctive message. In contrast to the way in which he is portrayed in other gospels, particularly New Testament gospels, Jesus in the Gospel of Thomas performs no physical miracles, reveals no fulfillment of prophecy, announces no apocalyptic kingdom about to disrupt the world order, and dies for no one's sins. Instead, Thomas's Jesus dispenses insight from the bubbling spring of wisdom (saying 13), discounts the value of prophecy and its fulfillment (saying 52), critiques end-of-the-world, apocalyptic announcements (sayings 51, 113), and offers a way of salvation through an encounter with the sayings of 'the living Jesus.'"

—Marvin Meyer, The Gospel of Thomas: The Hidden Sayings of Jesus (New York: Harper San Francisco, 1992), p. 10

25 Jesus said: Love your brother as your own soul.
Protect him as you protect the pupil of your eye.[13]

26 Jesus said: You see the splinter in your brother's eye,
but you do not see the log that is in your own eye.
Remove the log from your own eye, and then
you can clearly see to remove the splinter
from your brother's eye.[14]

15 Since the Kingdom of Heaven is already available on the earth within and outside people, they should become able to see it through their own inner light. What then of the former world, the world of fallenness and of religious obligations and prayer and repentance and so forth? That world needs to be put aside. Instead, one should radiate light into the world and receive that light back from the Kingdom. Accordingly, the less one interacts with the common perspectives of the world, the more one may come to see it in the new light of the Kingdom of Heaven. Thus, one should fast from the world as it ordinarily is in order to find the world to be the Kingdom of Heaven.

16 The practice of keeping the Sabbath is also a form of fasting, for to keep the Sabbath one refrains from work, just as one refrains from food in order to fast. It seems unlikely that Thomas's Gospel affirms the necessity of keeping standard Jewish religious conventions here, but speaks out against them in saying 14. Rather, the Thomasine community probably understood the Sabbath as a transformed way of interacting with the world, just as it understood fasting that way. So as one fasts from the world, so also one "Sabbaths" from the world.

Thomas probably has in mind the Sabbath of the Beginning, the Sabbath of the seventh day (Genesis 2:1–3), when God rested and blessed the seventh day and hallowed it. In accordance with the mythological thinking Thomas employs, after the Fall the first creation did not cease to exist, but it did become difficult to recognize. It must be sought and found. The Sabbath of the seventh day did not cease; it is the continuing state of the world-as-Kingdom, and perfected seven-day-old children dwell in that Sabbath. To find this state and live in it is the goal of the Gospel of Thomas.

27a If you do not fast from the world you will not find the Kingdom.[15]

27b If you do not keep the Sabbath as a Sabbath you will never see the Father.[16]

17 If you have a special relationship with the supernatural, you are going to have a much greater chance of convincing others of that fact if you are somewhere away from home rather than where you grew up. That common sense applies to Jesus, who was a prophet and a healer. Such people would be more successful among strangers, and this proverb attests to that fact.

The author of the Gospel of Mark created a life of Jesus from the sources available to him, few of which were narratives. One of Mark's principal sources was the sayings of Jesus, which he may have taken from some written texts as well as from oral tradition. Mark set out to construct a biography partially from isolated decontextualized sayings. We can follow him doing so as he creates his Gospel's chapter 6:1–6 from this proverb, writing of Jesus' return to his home town, their rejection of him as a prophet, his failure to heal those who knew him, and then concluding with Jesus speaking a version of this very saying.

18 This saying urges strength in defense while at the same time encouraging openness. You should not try to protect yourself by hiding your light, but at the same time you should be aware that attacks are likely. Ultimately you will be safe, above real danger, even if you expose yourself and your light to the world.

19 The first part of this saying shows that the Thomas sayings were not to be kept secret but transmitted widely. They are sometimes called secret sayings, but that is because their meanings are obscure and hard to figure out. The sayings themselves are public and should be preached from housetops. Saying 33b became a proverb in English-speaking lands, for everyone knows that "you shouldn't hide your light under a bushel."

31 Jesus said: No prophet is accepted in his own village. No physician heals the people who know him well.[17]

32 Jesus said: A city built and fortified atop a tall hill cannot be taken, nor can it be hidden.[18]

33a Jesus said: What you hear in your ears preach from your housetops.

33b For nobody lights a lamp and puts it underneath a bushel basket or in a hidden place. Rather, it is placed on a lamp stand so that all who go in and out may see the light.[19]

20 This saying is very similar to a comment about the Wisdom of God found in the Jewish book entitled *The Wisdom of Jesus ben Sirach* (also known as Ecclesiasticus): "Put your neck under her yoke, and let your souls receive instruction; it is to be found close by. See with your own eyes that I have labored but little and found for myself much serenity" (51:26–27). Here, in saying 90, a well-known expression appropriate to God's Wisdom is attributed to Jesus. In doing so, the Gospel of Thomas has Jesus speaking about himself as God's Wisdom.

"Rest" here seems to be a condition attainable in the present rather than an "eternal rest" to be obtained after death. In the Bible, the Letter to the Hebrews most prominently and repeatedly discusses "rest" as a reward for Christians, making the point that this kind of "rest" originates in the seventh-day rest of God in the week of the Beginning (Hebrews 4:8–12).

21 This is one of the sayings that most clearly express the unique perspectives of the Gospel of Thomas. The questioners represent those who would focus their attention on the person of Jesus himself, evidently assuming that what came to be known as "faith in Christ" is the proper essence of Christianity. In other words, they are seeking not to find the mystery of the Kingdom but the identity of Jesus himself.

They assume that Jesus primarily taught about himself. The Gospel of John shows him doing exactly that, for it is based on the principle that knowing who Jesus is (i.e., that he has come from the Father) is the essence of Christian faith and that Jesus continually tried to answer the demand "Tell us who you are so that we can believe in you." The Gospel of Thomas has no respect for this approach. In Thomas, when Jesus is asked about himself, he answers in terms of the whole world, deflecting attention from himself to the condition of reality.

90 Jesus said: Come to me. My yoke is easy. My mastery is gentle, and you will find rest for yourselves.[20]

91 They said to him: Tell us who you are so that we can believe in you. He replied: You analyze the appearance of the sky and the earth, but you don't recognize what is right in front of you, and you don't know the nature of the present time.[21]

4 □ Ramakrishna

Sri Ramakrishna in samadhi *during devotional singing at Keshab Sen's house. (The Master is supported by his nephew Hriday.)*

Walking with Ramakrishna ☐

If I had to choose one book to take with me to a desert island to con-
template for the rest of my life, or pick one book to give to a seeker today
to help guide him or her into the joys and mysteries of the mystical life, it
would be *The Gospel of Sri Ramakrishna*. It was written in Bengali at the
beginning of the twentieth century by Mahendra Gupta, a high school
headmaster from Calcutta, under the pseudonym M. It's a precise,
poignant, breathtakingly natural and candid account of a part of the life
and teachings of his beloved master Sri Ramakrishna, whose life
(1836–1886), lived mostly in the compound of a Kali temple by the side
of the Ganges, revolutionized religious history.

The Gospel of Sri Ramakrishna is the mystical equivalent of Boswell's
Life of Dr. Johnson: it is far more than a biography; it is a kind of living
transmission of the essence of the man himself, a "conjuration" of his
flaming living presence that time and cultural distance can never dim.
Swami Nikhilananda, whose English translation of the *Gospel* was first
published in 1942, considered these the first recorded words in the spiritual history of the world of a man recognized as belonging in the class of
a Buddha or a Christ. To read *The Gospel of Sri Ramakrishna* is to enter
into a dance with the great mystic; with the One constantly driving him
on; and, perhaps most mysteriously and challengingly of all, into a dance
with your own hidden innermost self, revealed in one of its wildest and
most generous incarnations. No one who meets with their whole being
the small brown man with the short beard and half-shut, obliquely set
eyes that these pages celebrate will ever be the same.

I first encountered this small man who has changed my life and influenced every step of my journey in the profoundest way when I was

twenty-five. I can still remember the afternoon on which I began to read M's book. I was seated at a table in a small hut by the sea in Pondicherry, in South India, gazing out at the sun shimmering in explosions of heat on the water. I had escaped the cage of an Oxford fellowship to return to drink deep from the springs of my Indian childhood and try to recover from the radiation of years of intellectual futility and emotional despair. Just two weeks before, I had undergone the first three of a series of mystical experiences that had shattered everything that I had ever understood or been taught about reality: I had been left charred, profoundly afraid that I would lose my mind. And then a friend handed me *The Gospel of Sri Ramakrishna* and told me to read it immediately. "You will find in this book everything you will ever need. You are not going mad, you are going sane."

I started reading the *Gospel* around noon; at seven, as fragrant night fell over the sea, I was still reading, transfixed and strangely calm. I was far from understanding, of course, much of what I read, but I knew that in Ramakrishna, I had met the most tender and amazing friend, someone whose wisdom and perception would always be ready to encourage my own. In beginning to read the work of another great Hindu mystic, Aurobindo, I had already started to open tentatively to a wholly new (to me) vision of God as Mother; now, reading and experiencing Ramakrishna, I realized with awe and delight that the meaning of my whole life would be connected to the vision of the Mother I met in and through him. I realized too that, as I deepened my experience of the Mother, I would also deepen my experience of Ramakrishna, of what he had been and done and of what he was still doing to and in the heart of humanity. When I put down the *Gospel* toward midnight, too exhausted to continue, I knew that everything had changed forever for me.

Nine years later, after I had read and reread *The Gospel of Sri Ramakrishna* countless times—and, inspired by it, entered into an exploration of God as Mother and of the essence of all mystical traditions—I went on pilgrimage to the place where Ramakrishna had lived, the Kali Temple, in Dakshineshwar, six miles outside of Calcutta. I sat in the serene radiance of his simple room, near the Ganges, for most of the day, and then caught a bus back to Calcutta. On the bus, I began to panic. I had no real idea where my hotel was or where the bus was going. In the immense filthy labyrinth of the city I started to pray to Ramakrishna. Five minutes later, I heard a rather high-pitched voice say in accented Indian-English, "Get out now." I looked around; no one was sitting near me. I left the bus; my hotel was thirty yards away. With tears of astonishment, I understood that the small brown man had spoken directly to me and that he would always be there to guide and direct me whenever my life re-entered chaos.

I tell this story here because when I have told it to those of my spiritual friends who love Ramakrishna, they answer with their own accounts of his miraculous presence and guidance. Ramakrishna is a world-teacher in the company of Jesus and Rumi and the Buddha, transcendentally alive as they are, and tangible in the heart, as a permanently empowered "emanation" of the Beloved. I have kept a photograph of him in ecstasy (the same one that is on page 130) on my desk for twenty-five years and I look into his eyes every day to remind myself of what I must try, with all my fractures and differences, to become. In times of great difficulty and torment, I have found in his company inexplicable grace and peace. At a certain juncture on the path, you discover that all the great healers and teachers and mystics of humanity are waiting behind a razor-thin veil of light to meet you and help you help others. The unveiling of this mystery of communion between all lovers of God and of the world beyond time and death is one of the holiest of revelations and one of the most useful; the responsibilities of the later stages of the path would often be unfathomable and lonely without it.

There has never been a time in which humanity needed Ramakrishna's holy company and inspiration more. The next decade will decide the fate of humankind and of much of nature. Those whose eyes have been opened see that we are all heading into a whirlwind of catastrophe, war, heartbreak on the one hand, and, on the other, of unprecedented opportunities for real transformation on a massive, world-altering scale. This time will not come again in all its terrible grace; those of us who are becoming awake have no other choice but to seize it with all the strength of our sometimes-shattered hearts and minds.

I believe that the guidance, example, and vision of Ramakrishna are essential to human survival for three linked reasons. They unfold a uniquely rich understanding of the power and splendor of the Divine Mother, of her all-transforming grace, and of the unity in her complete love and knowledge of all religions and mystical revelations. They expose a direct path to her that anyone in any culture or of any religious, economic, social, or sexual persuasion can take to her, and they make gloriously plain the abundant, fertile life she will give to all those who turn to her in adoration and humble trust. Ramakrishna birthed in his own heart, body, mind, and soul the New World of the Motherhood of God that is trying now to be born on a massive scale in the holocaust of history. His life, teachings, and vision are the sign that transfiguration is not poetic illusion or the last-ditch fantasy of a few mystics, but a living and breathing reality, one infinitely wilder, sweeter, richer, and more all-embracing than anything any previous revelations of human potential had imagined. Ramakrishna is the pioneer of the real New Age, when living divine children are nurtured by the Motherhood of God; his closeness to us in time and the astonished but precise testimony of M and his other disciples make his challenge to us inescapable. As Lex Hixon wrote in his introduction to *Great Swan: Meetings with Ramakrishna,* "Ramakrishna is not a quaint person from an ancient culture, representing a particular religious background, but an Einstein of the planetary civilization of the near future, a greenhouse for the future evolution of humanity."

That Ramakrishna became "a greenhouse for the future evolution of humanity" was entirely due—and he himself claims this—to his lifelong devotion to the Motherhood of God. Ramakrishna came to know and

understand that he had a unique mission to humanity: to unfold the revelations and possibilities that lay open to all who invoke and adore the
Divine Mother in any of her names or forms. From his earliest childhood,
Ramakrishna had a passion for the Mother; as a boy, Swami Saradananda
tells us in his *Sri Ramakrishna, the Great Master,* "Ramakrishna gave up
going to school and applied his mind to the worship of the Devi. But
where was peace even in that? His mind questioned, 'Is it true that the
universal Mother is the embodiment of bliss and not a mere stone image?
Or is it a superstition of the human mind, augmented by fond imagination
and tradition of ages that has produced this unreal shadowy figure? And
has man thus been deceiving himself from time immemorial?' His mind
became extremely eager to solve that great problem'" (2:771).

The unfolding of his life—and of her in and through him—became
the overwhelming answer to this "great problem." Not long after
Ramakrishna came to live in the compound of Rani Rasmani's temple of
Kali at Dakshineswar in his late teens, he began the most comprehensive journey into the Motherhood of God that the world has seen.
Absolute trust in and devotion to the Mother led him from stage to stage
of ecstasy, empowerment, and revelation of her nature in all its dazzling
and paradoxical formal and formless aspects until, at last, he came to
know her to be as inseparable from Brahman the absolute reality "as
burning is from fire."

For him, the entire cosmos in all of its infinite grandeur and tiniest
details became a never-ending epiphany of the Mother. Swami
Saradananda reports Ramakrishna as saying, "I see as if all trees, plants,
men, grass, water and other things are only sheaths of various kinds.
They are like pillowcases. Have you not seen them? Some are made of
coarse cotton cloth dyed red, some of chintz, and others of different
kinds of cloth; and in size, some are quadrangular, others circular. The
Universe is just so ...again, just as the same thing, namely cotton, is stuffed
into all these pillowcases, so that one invisible Existence-Knowledge-Bliss
dwells within all the sheaths. My children, for me, it is actually as if the

Mother has covered herself with wrappers of various kinds or hidden behind various forms, and is peeping out from within them all"(*Sri Ramakrishna, the Great Master,* 2:675). This revelation of the Mother in and as everything was the gift of six months of total absorption in her in 1864, when Ramakrishna was twenty-eight, in the highest, nondual bliss known as *nirvikalpa Samadhi.* In the Hindu mystical tradition, it is said that such a state destroys the body, or necessitates the soul's abandonment of its "sheath" after only three weeks; Ramakrishna was kept alive by the help of a mysterious monk who fed him the barest minimum for his body's survival. When he "came down" from this prolonged ecstasy, he was transfigured and visibly divinely empowered. The Mother herself, it is said, asked him to remain in *bhavamukha*—at the threshold of relative and absolute consciousness—so as to be able to teach, embody, and witness her reality.

It was in this extraordinary state of unity that Ramakrishna then proceeded on what remains the most revolutionary aspect of his journey: his diving first into the depths of Islam toward the end of 1866, when, with the help of a Sufi adept, he realized union with Allah; and then, eight years later, in November 1874, his plunging into Christianity. After three days of absorption in Christ, he met and merged into him in the garden of Dakshineswar. From these two immense experiences (and those that preceded them), Ramakrishna became the first known prophet in history to proclaim the essential unity of all religions, thus pointing the way to the end of all division and war in the name of religion and pioneering a new planetary civilization, in which all faiths would be honored as complementary and distinct paths to God, different "dishes" in the heavenly and merciful cuisine of the Mother for her children. As Ramakrishna said, "God has made different religions to suit different aspirations, times and countries . . . as a mother in nursing her sick children gives rice and curry to one, and sago and arrowroot to another, and bread and butter to a third, so the Lord has laid out different paths for different people." The potential value of this vision—of all paths and revelations unified in the

Mother—is incalculable; only an undivided humankind can solve the economic, political, and environmental problems that menace all life, and humankind can only be undivided if religions that are now the source of strife give up their ignorant claims of exclusiveness.

Ramakrishna did not merely experience this revelation of unity: he pointed out a direct path to its realization that beings of all cultures or belief structures could take. The fabulous richness and range of his own experience gave him inner knowledge of the many ways of approaching God, with or without form; and his own constant experience of the direct grace of the Mother convinced him that anyone who turned to her—as he had—with total trust and belief would be fed—as he had been—directly by her, with everything they would need to become her illumined servants of radical love.

This was a revolutionary position, one that implicitly challenged millennia of priestly control and guru-worship. Those who claim Ramakrishna as a guru figure limit him. He was, of course, the most magical and lucid of teachers. But he was also something more mysterious—a living, divine child of the Mother who pointed a way of direct connection to her that could help all others who sincerely and ardently wanted it to birth themselves in her. He himself hated being called a "guru," for he knew that the Mother and her inner guide within every heart are the only real "gurus," and his experience of her had taken him far beyond the need for any kind of authority, even one he claimed to be "divine"; in this way too Ramakrishna's example was prophetic. As the religious and mystical structures of authority crumble around us, Ramakrishna's discovery and embodiment of the direct path will become more and more empowering. As he said, "The substance is one under different names, and everyone is seeing the same substance: only climate, temperament and name create differences. Let each man follow his own path. If he sincerely and ardently wishes to know God, peace be unto him, he will surely realize him." Ramakrishna's own journey began and ended with only one teacher: the Mother herself. On his way he embraced and learned deeply from several adepts but ultimately absorbed and transcended all they had to offer him. He gives all modern seekers a deathless example of the necessary dance between respectful but not slavish dependence and fundamental independence in and under God that the fullest realizations necessitate.

If Ramakrishna had only left humanity the vision of the all-unifying Motherhood of God and the direct path to her, he would have permanently changed religious history. But through the divine agency of his disciple M he did something even more astonishing: he left us, in M's pages, a permanent and exuberantly beautiful image of the life that abandon to the Mother brings. The ecstatic and lucid being that haunts the pages of M's *Gospel* is someone who has fused at ever-increasing depths of sacred truth, and passion, all possible human and divine opposites, masculine and feminine, to birth in himself the sacred Divine Child, and to manifest the miraculous powers of clarity and rapture that dance and keep dancing from such a birth. M's Ramakrishna is at once intensely human and divine, at once childlike and innocent and majestic. No realm of vision is closed to him; no secret does not stand open to his gaze, and no tenderness is beneath him. He is as much his divine self laughing with his heart-friends on a boat or at a supper party as he is drowned in silence or speaking with divinely inspired clarity the essential truths of the path.

There is a description of Ramakrishna dancing by Swami Saradananda that perfectly captures the mystery of his infinitely subtle negotiation and marriage of all levels of reality: "An extraordinary tenderness, sweetness and leonine strength were visible in every limb of the Master's body. That superb dance! In it there was no artificiality or affectation, no bumping, no unnatural gestures and acrobatics; nor was there to be noticed any absence of control. On the other hand, one noticed in it a succession of natural poses and movements of limbs as a gushing overflow of grace, bliss and sweetness surging from within, the like of which may be noticed in the movements of a large fish, long confined in a mud puddle when it is suddenly let loose in a vast sheet of water—swimming in all directions, now slowly, now rapidly, and expressing its joy in diverse ways. It appeared as if the dance was the dynamically bodily expression of the surge of bliss, the reality of Brahman, which the Master was experiencing within" (2:801). If we do not embody this dance of the Mother, with "extraordinary tenderness, sweetness and leonine strength" at all levels and in all institutions, the world will die out. In the sublime interconnected dance of Ramakrishna's teachings, life and vision, we are given the music we need to move to, a vision of the divine choreography that we need to reimagine for our own lives, and an eternal sign of the power of her love in us that can transform, endure, and transfigure all things.

In the unabridged version of *The Gospel of Sri Ramakrishna*, the Master describes the passion that grew in him after his experience of the Mother was complete and he could share its wonders with others: "When, during the evening service, the temples rang with the sound of bells and conch shells, I would climb to the roof of the *kuthi* [the bungalow] of the garden and, writhing in anguish of heart, cry at the top of my voice 'Come my children! Oh, where are you? I cannot bear to live without you!' A mother never longed so intensely for the sight of her child, nor a friend for his companions, nor a lover for his sweetheart, as I longed for them." Ramakrishna is still crying out to us from the heart of the Mother. On how many of us, and how deeply we respond to him and his example, will depend a good part of our survival.

মাস্টার—ঈশ্বরকে কি দর্শন করা যায় ?

শ্রীরামকৃষ্ণ—হাঁ, অবশ্য করা যায়। মাঝে মাঝে নির্জনে বাস; তাঁর নাম-গুণগান, বস্তু-বিচার; এইসব উপায় অবলম্বন করতে হয়।

মাস্টার—কি অবস্থাতে তাঁকে দর্শন হয় ?

শ্রীরামকৃষ্ণ—খুব ব্যাকুল হয়ে কাঁদলে তাঁকে দেখা যায়। মাগছেলের জন্য লোকে এক ঘটি কাঁদে; টাকার জন্য লোকে কেঁদে ভাসিয়ে দেয়; কিন্তু ঈশ্বরের জন্য কে কাঁদছে ? তাকার মত ডাকলে হয়।

A portion of The Gospel of Sri Ramakrishna
in the original Bengali script

Ramakrishna and
The Gospel of Sri Ramakrishna □

Kendra Crossen Burroughs

It has been said that one moment in the company of an enlightened master is more valuable than a hundred years of sincere worship. Relatively few people ever get the opportunity to meet a man or woman of the highest realization. Yet so powerful is the influence of these great souls that even a written account of what it is like to be in their presence can impart to us the fragrance of their divine companionship.

The Gospel of Sri Ramakrishna is such an account. Well over a century after his death, Sri Ramakrishna (1836–1886) is still capturing hearts and making them long for the truth of divine life, through this classic record of his encounters with disciples and devotees. Because the full-length book is very long and sometimes daunting for newcomers, this collection of annotated excerpts is offered as an entrée into the world of this unique spiritual personality.

Sri Ramakrishna's ecstatic mystical states, the wisdom and humor of his storytelling, his childlike purity, and his expression of both the masculine and feminine energies of divine love are just a few of the qualities, reflected in this book, that make him so appealing. In particular, he is recognized worldwide for his message that all religions are paths to the truth. Of all the noteworthy spiritual leaders produced by India in the modern era, Sri Ramakrishna seems to have played a special role in heralding the movement toward harmony and tolerance in our time. Although at present the world appears engulfed in religious conflict, the seed of unity planted by Ramakrishna must eventually bear its fruit.

Sri Ramakrishna (*Sri,* pronounced *Shree,* is an honorific title) was born Gadadhar Chatterjee in a remote village of the Bengali-speaking region of eastern India now known as West Bengal. His parents were poor brahmins, the highest-ranking social group in the Hindu caste system, traditionally associated with the occupations of teacher and priest. A sensitive child with talent in devotional singing, acting in religious dramas, and making images of deities, Gadadhar received a simple village education and also learned the formal rituals of worship at a young age. At sixteen he traveled to Calcutta to assist his eldest brother, Ramkumar, in his duties as a priest. Within a few years, they began serving at a large new temple complex in the nearby village of Dakshineshwar, Ramkumar becoming priest of the temple of Kali—the great goddess known as the Divine Mother—while Gadadhar was appointed to one of the smaller shrines. When Ramkumar fell ill and died in 1856, Gadadhar assumed the role of priest to the Divine Mother. From this time, the young man's already fervent inner life began to intensify as he plunged into a quest of desperate spiritual longing that would transform him into the God-intoxicated sage revered as Ramakrishna.

He began to spend long periods in solitary meditation and sometimes neglected his formal duties while he lost himself in singing ecstatically before the temple image of Kali. In her he experienced the all-loving Mother of the Universe, despite her frightening appearance. A fierce black figure, her hair in wild disarray and her tongue protruding from her mouth, Kali has four arms: one hand holds a bloody sword, another the decapitated head of a demon, and the other two make gestures of blessing and reassurance to her worshipers. She wears a garland of human skulls and a girdle made of severed arms. A symbol of the feminine power that energizes all masculine divinity, she stands on the corpse of her husband, Shiva. To this awesome goddess, bestower of both life and death, blessings and misfortunes, Ramakrishna wept and prayed, begging for a vision of her reality.

When his desperation reached its peak, his prayer was granted, and the Mother revealed herself as the infinite, effulgent Ocean of Bliss—the first of many visions of Divinity he was to experience. In the phase of spiritual intoxication that followed, Ramakrishna's behavior—including such sacrilegious acts as feeding a cat with food meant as an offering to the Goddess—appeared outrageous to some. Others, however, accepted his madness as evidence of his realization, for he now directly saw the presence of the Mother at play in all things.

With the idea that marriage might "cure" him, Ramakrishna was encouraged to wed, and at age twenty-three he was betrothed to a five-year-old girl of his own choosing, named Sarada. According to custom, such a marriage would be consummated when the bride reached puberty, but this was never to occur in the case of Ramakrishna and Sarada. Although she eventually came to live with her husband at Dakshineshwar, it was as his spiritual companion and disciple, and he in turn treated her as a living manifestation of the Divine Mother.

In the meantime, Ramakrishna's inner journey continued to unfold through a series of unusual spiritual experiments. In 1861 he came into contact with the first of several gurus, a woman master of Tantra under whose guidance his divine frenzy was transformed into the joyous attitude of a child delighting in the blissful play created by his Mother. It was this guru who first declared Ramakrishna to be an avatar, a direct manifestation of God in human form. Two of the signs of this status, accepted by religious authorities, were said to be his ability to remain for long periods in a state of divine absorption and the power of granting spiritual awakening through his touch.

Over the next several years, Ramakrishna worshiped the Divine under different names and forms—as the avatars Rama and Krishna, as the formless Brahman of Vedanta philosophy, as the God of Islam, and as Jesus Christ. Through his own inner experiences of the truths taught by various sects and creeds, Ramakrishna became a living embodiment of the essence of all true religion. His life itself was his gospel of unity amid diversity.

In time Sri Ramakrishna began to attract wider public notice, and people flocked to his little room in the temple garden overlooking the Ganges River. At the feet of this humble village priest, who spoke in simple vernacular language, sat scholars of Sanskrit, Western-educated Bengali intellectuals, and wealthy landowners as well as ordinary people. The conversations recounted in *The Gospel of Sri Ramakrishna*—recorded by one of the participants, Mahendranath Gupta (referred to in the text as "M" or Mahendra)—took place among the Master's male devotees and disciples, but he had a devoted group of female followers as well. The streams of visitors were entranced by his homespun parables, his profound spiritual knowledge, and the awe-inspiring accounts of his visions. And now and then, as the Master drifted into the state of divine absorption known as *samadhi,* they simply basked in the beauty of his presence.

Sri Ramakrishna's most beloved disciple, Swami Vivekananda, once posed the question of how we are to recognize a true teacher. The Master gave this answer:

> In the first place, the sun requires no torch to make it visible. We do not light a candle to see the sun. When the sun rises, we instinctively become aware of its rising; and when a teacher of men comes to help us, the soul will instinctively know that it has found the truth. Truth stands on its own evidences; it does not require any other testimony to attest it; it is self-effulgent. It penetrates into the innermost recesses of our nature, and the whole universe stands up and says, "This is the Truth."

That radiant presence is here now, as you turn these pages.

Selections from
The Gospel of
Sri Ramakrishna

Courtesy of Ramakrishna-Vivekananda Center of New York

The Dakshineshwar temples seen from the sacred Ganges River

1 The *gunas* are the three primary qualities of nature. *Sattva* is variously described as being, consciousness, tranquility, balance, and truth. *Rajas* is the dynamic principle of desire, attachment, change, and activity. *Tamas* is inertia, darkness, and ignorance. All that exists or occurs is a result of the interplay of these three forces, which combine in different ways to produce everything in nature. Even modern science might be said to acknowlesdge this ancient truth of three forces, in the form of Newton's three laws of motion and the three laws of thermodynamics. *Bhakti* is the path of devotion.

146

☐ Dive Deep

MASTER: "Many people visit the temple garden at Dakshineshwar. If I see some among the visitors indifferent to God, I say to them, 'You had better sit over there.' Or sometimes I say, 'Go and see the beautiful buildings.' (*Laughter*)

"Sometimes I find that the devotees of God are accompanied by worthless people. Their companions are immersed in gross worldliness and don't enjoy spiritual talk at all. Since the devotees keep on, for a long time, talking with me about God, the others become restless. Finding it impossible to sit there any longer, they whisper to their devotee friends: 'When shall we be going? How long will you stay here?' The devotees say: 'Wait a bit. We shall go after a little while.' Then the worldly people say in a disgusted tone: 'Well, then, you can talk. We shall wait for you in the boat.' (*All laugh.*)

"Worldly people will never listen to you if you ask them to renounce everything and devote themselves wholeheartedly to God. As worldly people are endowed with sattva, rajas, and tamas, so also is bhakti characterized by the three gunas.[1]

"Do you know what a worldly person endowed with sattva is like? Perhaps his house is in a dilapidated condition here and there. He doesn't care to repair it. The worship hall may be strewn with pigeon droppings and the courtyard covered with moss, but he pays no attention to these things. The furniture of the house may be old; he doesn't think of polishing it and making it look neat. He doesn't care for dress at all; anything is good enough for him. But the man himself is very gentle, quiet, kind, and humble; he doesn't injure anyone.

2 *Tilak* is a mark on the forehead, made with a substance such as sandalwood paste, ashes, or red turmeric powder, to indicate what religious sect one belongs to.

3 *Rudraksha* are the dried berries of the tree *Elaeocarpus ganitrus,* used as beads for rosaries *(malas),* especially by devotees of Shiva. Usually there are 108 beads on a strand, for counting mantra recitations. *Rudraksha* are credited with various auspicious and healing powers and the ability to dispel sins.

4 A *dacoit* is a member of a gang of robbers.

"Again, among the worldly there are people with the traits of rajas. Such a man has a watch and chain, and two or three rings on his fingers. The furniture of his house is all spick and span. On the walls hang portraits of the Queen, the Prince of Wales, and other prominent people; the building is whitewashed and spotlessly clean. His wardrobe is filled with a large assortment of clothes; even the servants have their livery and all that.

"The traits of a worldly man endowed with tamas are sleep, lust, anger, egotism, and the like.

"Similarly, bhakti, devotion, may be sattvic. A devotee who possesses it meditates on God in absolute secret, perhaps inside his mosquito net. Others think he is asleep. Since he is late in getting up, they think perhaps he has not slept well during the night. His love for the body goes only as far as appeasing his hunger, and that also by means of rice and simple greens. There is no elaborate arrangement about his meals, no luxury in clothes, and no display of furniture. Besides, such a devotee never flatters anybody for money.

"An aspirant possessed of rajasic bhakti puts a tilak[2] on his forehead and a necklace of holy rudraksha[3] beads, interspersed with gold ones, around his neck. (*All laugh.*) At worship he wears a silk cloth. He likes outer display.

"A man endowed with tamasic bhakti has burning faith. Such a devotee literally extorts boons from God, even as a robber falls upon a man and plunders his money. 'Bind! Beat! Kill!'—that is his way, the way of the dacoits."[4]

Saying this, the Master began to sing in a voice sweet with rapturous love, his eyes turned upward:

5 The places named are all pilgrimage sites. Ganga is the Indian name for the river Ganges. The holy city Kashi is also known as Varanasi.

6 It is said (for example, in the Bhagavad Gita) that whatever thought the mind holds at the time of death will determine one's future existence. Most auspicious would be to think of God or repeat a divine name while dying.

7 The three holy hours are dawn, noon, and dusk.

8 Madan is the name of the poet who wrote the song.

9 Shiva is often shown with five faces and many arms, a symbol of his omnipotence.

Why should I go to Gaya or Ganga, to Kashi, Kanchi, or
Prabhas,[5]
So long as I can breathe my last with Kali's name upon my lips?[6]
What need of worship has a man, what need of rituals anymore,
If he repeats the Mother's name during the three holy hours?[7]
Rituals may pursue him close, but they can never overtake him.
Charity, vows, and giving of gifts have no appeal for Madan's[8]
mind;
The Blissful Mother's Lotus Feet are his prayer and sacrifice.
Who could ever have conceived the power Her holy name
possesses?
Shiva Himself, the God of gods, sings Her praise with His five
mouths.[9]

The Master was beside himself with love for the Divine Mother. He
said, "One must take the firm attitude: 'What? I have chanted the
Mother's name. How can I be a sinner anymore? I am Her child, heir
to Her powers and glories.'

"If you can give a spiritual turn to your tamas, you can realize God
with its help. Force your demands on God. He is by no means a
stranger to you. He is indeed your very own.

"Furthermore, you see, the quality of tamas can be used for the
welfare of others. There are three classes of physicians: superior,
mediocre, and inferior. The physician who feels the patient's pulse
and just says to him, 'Take the medicine regularly,' belongs to the
inferior class. He doesn't care to inquire whether or not the patient
has actually taken the medicine. The mediocre physician is he who in
various ways persuades the patient to take the medicine and says to
him sweetly: 'My good man, how will you be cured unless you use the
medicine? Take this medicine. I have prepared it for you myself.' But
he who, finding the patient stubbornly refusing to take the medicine, forces it down his throat, going so far as to put his knee on the

10 The *bhakta* is a follower of the path of devotion, and the *jnani* is a follower of the path of knowledge.

11 Brahman is God in the absolute state, beyond imagination and conception. Because Brahman is formless, It is distinguished from the personal forms of God worshiped by the world religions; however, in reality It is inseparable from the personal God, because according to Advaita (Nondualistic) Vedanta philosophy, Brahman is Existence in its entirety, One without a second.

@ "It is not good to say that what we ourselves think of God is the only truth and what others think is false; that because we think of God as formless, therefore He is formless and cannot have any form; that because we think of God as having form, therefore He has form and cannot be formless. Can a man really fathom God's nature?

"I see people who talk about religion constantly quarreling with one another. Hindus, Mussalmans, Brahmos, Shaktas, Vaishnavas, Shaivas, all quarrel with one another. They haven't the intelligence to understand that He who is called Krishna is also Shiva and the Primal Shakti, and that it is He, again, who is called Jesus and Allah. 'There is only one Rama and He has a thousand names.' Truth is one; It is only called by different names. All people are seeking the same Truth; the disagreement is due to differences in climate, temperament, and names. Everyone is going toward God. They will all realize Him if they have sincerity and longing of heart."

—Sri Ramakrishna *[299–300]*

patient's chest, is the best physician. This is the manifestation of tamas in the physician. It doesn't injure the patient; on the contrary, it does him good.

"Like the physicians, there are three types of religious teachers. The inferior teacher only gives instruction to the student but makes no inquiries about his progress. The mediocre teacher, for the good of the student, makes repeated efforts to bring the instruction home to him, begs him to assimilate it, and shows his fondness for him in many other ways. But there is a type of teacher who goes to the length of using force when he finds the student persistently unyielding; I call him the best teacher."

A BRAHMO DEVOTEE: "Sir, has God forms or has He none?"

MASTER: "No one can say with finality that God is only 'this' and nothing else. He is formless, and again He has forms. For the bhakta He assumes forms. But He is formless for the jnani[10], that is, for him who looks on the world as a mere dream. The bhakta feels that he is one entity and the world another. Therefore God reveals Himself to him as a Person. But the jnani—the Vedantist, for instance—always reasons, applying the process of 'Not this, not this.' Through this discrimination he realizes, by inner perception, that the ego and the universe are both illusory, like a dream. Then the jnani realizes Brahman[11] in his own consciousness. He cannot describe what Brahman is.

"Do you know what I mean? Think of Brahman, Existence-Knowledge-Bliss Absolute, as a shoreless ocean. Through the cooling influence, as it were, of the bhakta's love, the water has frozen at places into blocks of ice. In other words, God now and then assumes various forms for His lovers and reveals Himself to them as a Person. But with the rising of the sun of Knowledge, the blocks of ice melt. Then one doesn't feel anymore that God is a Person, nor does one see God's forms. What He is cannot be described. Who will describe

@ "I have observed that a man acquires one kind of knowledge about God through reasoning and another kind through meditation; but he acquires a third kind of knowledge about God when God reveals Himself to him, His devotee. If God Himself reveals to His devotee the nature of Divine Incarnation—how He plays in human form—then the devotee doesn't have to reason about the problem or need an explanation. Do you know what it is like? Suppose a man is in a dark room. He goes on rubbing a match against a matchbox and all of a sudden light comes. Likewise, if God gives us this flash of divine light, all our doubts are destroyed. Can one ever know God by mere reasoning?"

—Sri Ramakrishna *[377]*

12 God with attributes (Saguna Brahman) is the personal God, Lord (Ishvara) of the Universe. God in the absolute state, without attributes (Nirguna Brahman), transcends personal qualities.

Him? He who would do so disappears. He cannot find his 'I' anymore.

"If one analyzes oneself, one doesn't find any such thing as 'I.' Take an onion, for instance. First of all you peel off the red outer skin; then you find thick white skins. Peel these off one after the other and you won't find anything inside.

"In that state a man no longer feels the existence of his ego. And who is there left to seek it? Who can describe how he feels in that state—in his own Pure Consciousness—about the real nature of Brahman?

"There is a sign of Perfect Knowledge. A man becomes silent when It is attained. Then the 'I,' which may be likened to a salt doll, melts in the Ocean of Existence-Knowledge-Bliss Absolute and becomes one with It. Not the slightest trace of distinction is left.

"As long as his self-analysis is not complete, man argues with much ado. But he becomes silent when he completes it. When the empty pitcher has been filled with water, when the water inside the pitcher becomes one with the water of the lake outside, no more sound is heard. Sound comes from the pitcher as long as the pitcher is not filled with water.

"All trouble and botheration come to an end when the 'I' dies. You may indulge in thousands of reasonings, but still the 'I' doesn't disappear. For people like you and me it is good to have the feeling, 'I am a lover of God.'

"The Saguna Brahman[12] is meant for the bhaktas. In other words, a bhakta believes that God has attributes and reveals Himself to men as a Person, assuming forms. It is He who listens to our prayers. The prayers that you utter are directed to Him alone. It doesn't matter whether you accept God with form or not. It is enough to feel that God is a person who listens to our prayers, who creates, preserves, and destroys the universe, and who is endowed with infinite power.

"It is easier to attain God by following the path of devotion."

Sri Ramakrishna was teaching the devotees how to call on the Divine Mother. "I used to pray to Her in this way: 'O Mother! O Blissful One! Reveal Thyself to me. Thou must!' Again, I would say to Her: 'O Lord of the lowly! O Lord of the universe! Surely I am not outside Thy universe. I am bereft of knowledge. I am without discipline. I have no devotion. I know nothing. Thou must be gracious and reveal Thyself to me.'"

—*The Gospel of Sri Ramakrishna [283]*

BRAHMO DEVOTEE: "Sir, is it possible for one to see God? If so, why can't we see Him?"

MASTER: "Yes, He can surely be seen. One can see His forms, and His formless aspects too. How can I explain that to you?"

BRAHMO DEVOTEE: "What are the means by which one can see God?"

MASTER: "Can you weep for Him with intense longing of heart? Men shed a jugful of tears for the sake of their children, for their wives, or for money. But who weeps for God? So long as the child remains engrossed with its toys, the mother looks after her cooking and other household duties. But when the child no longer relishes the toys, it throws them aside and yells for its mother. Then the mother puts the rice pot down from the hearth, runs in haste, and takes the child in her arms."

BRAHMO DEVOTEE: "Sir, why are there so many different opinions about God's nature? Some say that God has form, while others say that He is formless. Again, those who speak of God with form tell us about His different forms. Why all this controversy?"

MASTER: "A devotee thinks of God as he sees Him. In reality there is no confusion about God. God explains all this to the devotee if the devotee only somehow realizes Him. You haven't set your foot in that direction. How can you expect to know all about God?

"Listen to a story. Once a man entered a jungle and saw a small animal on a tree. He came back and told another man that he had seen a creature of a beautiful red color on a certain tree. The second man replied: 'When I went into the jungle, I too saw that animal. But why do you call it red? It is green.' Another man who was present contradicted them both and insisted that it was yellow. Presently others arrived and contended that it was gray, violet, blue, and so forth and so on. At last they started quarreling among themselves. To settle the dispute they all went to the tree. They saw a man sitting under

13 The fifteenth-century North Indian devotional poet Kabir is a famous mystic, revered by both Hindus and Muslims.

14 Shankaracharya says, "Only through God's grace may we obtain those three rarest advantages—human birth, the longing for liberation, and discipleship to an illumined teacher." Only as a human being can one strive for and attain liberation from the seemingly endless round of birth and death in illusion. Thus, Shankaracharya asks, "What greater fool can there be than the man who has obtained this rare human birth together with bodily and mental strength and yet fails, through delusion, to realize his own highest good?"

15 *Brahmajnani* means "knower of Brahman."

16 "Woman and gold" is a translation of the Bengali *kamini-kanchan*, in which the word *kamini* implies a seductress—it does not mean women in general. Sexual desire and greed or possessiveness were identified by Ramakrishna as the most binding obstacles to spiritual progress. Sri Ramakrishna did not mean that women are to "blame" for lust, nor did he teach his male devotees to hate women. On the contrary, he revered women as sacred representatives of the Goddess. Swami Nikhilananda notes that when Ramakrishna addressed his female devotees, he warned them against attachment to "man and gold."

17 Hindu cosmology views time as a cyclic process. The universe is created and dissolved many times, spanning vast time periods. In a cycle of creation, the world moves gradually through four cycles called *yugas*, during which conditions progressively deteriorate. Humanity is said to be now in the fourth period, the Kali Yuga, a dark age of ignorance and suffering. After this degenerate age culminates in dissolution, the world will spring forth anew into an age of enlightenment, the beginning of a new cycle. The date traditionally assigned to the beginning of the Kali Yuga is about 3000 B.C.E.

18 The planes of consiousness are correlated with centers of subtle energy *(prana)* in the body.

it. On being asked, he replied: 'Yes, I live under this tree and I know the animal very well. All your descriptions are true. Sometimes it appears red, sometimes yellow, and at other times blue, violet, gray, and so forth. It is a chameleon. And sometimes it has no color at all. Now it has a color, and now it has none.'

"In like manner, one who constantly thinks of God can know His real nature; he alone knows that God reveals Himself to seekers in various forms and aspects. God has attributes; then again He has none. Only the man who lives under the tree knows that the chameleon can appear in various colors, and he knows, further, that it at times has no color at all. It is the others who suffer from the agony of futile argument.

"Kabir[13] used to say, 'The formless Absolute is my Father, and God with form is my Mother.' God reveals Himself in the form which His devotee loves most. His love for the devotee knows no bounds.

"Yours is the path of bhakti. That is very good; it is an easy path. Who can fully know the infinite God? And what need is there of knowing the Infinite? Having attained this rare human birth,[14] my supreme need is to develop love for God's Lotus Feet.

"If a jug of water is enough to remove my thirst, why should I measure the quantity of water in a lake? Suppose a man gets drunk on half a bottle of wine: what is the use of his calculating the quantity of wine in the tavern? What need is there of knowing the Infinite?

"The various states of the Brahmajnani's[15] mind are described in the Vedas. The path of knowledge is extremely difficult. One cannot obtain jnana if one has the least trace of worldliness and the slightest attachment to 'woman' and 'gold.'[16] This is not the path for the Kali Yuga[17].

"The Vedas speak of seven planes where the mind can dwell. When the mind is immersed in worldliness it dwells in the three lower planes—at the navel, the organ of generation, and the organ of evacuation.[18] In that state the mind loses all its higher visions—it

@ "The spinal column is said to contain two nerve-currents, called *ida* and *pingala*. (These have been identified, I do not know how correctly, with the sensory and motor nerves of our Western physiology.) Ida is said to be on the left of the spinal column; pingala on the right. In the middle is a passage which is called the *sushumna*. When the kundalini is aroused, it passes up the sushumna; which otherwise, in the case of normally unspiritual people, remains closed. When Ramakrishna speaks of the centres of the navel, heart, throat, etc., he is using physical organs to indicate the approximate positions of these centres; actually, they are located within the sushumna itself.

"These centres are also often called 'lotuses' in Hindu writings on the subject, because they are said to appear in the form of a lotus to those whose spiritual vision enables them to see them. It is wrong to think of the centres as being gross physical organs; but it must be remembered, on the other hand, that Hindu physiology makes no sharp distinction between gross and subtle. It is all a question of degree.

"It was noticed that, in the case of Ramakrishna, the ascent of the kundalini was accompanied by a constant and powerful movement of the blood towards the chest and brain. In consequence of this, the skin of his chest was always flushed."

—Christopher Isherwood

19 In *samadhi* (sometimes translated as "trance"), the mind is merged with the Divine, so that there is no longer any separation between the subject (the meditator) and the object (God). When asked once how he felt in *samadhi*, Ramakrishna replied, "I feel like a fish released from a pot into the water of the Ganges."

20 *Japa* is the mental repetition of a mantra or a name of God as a meditation.

broods only on 'woman' and 'gold.' The fourth plane of the mind is at the heart. When the mind dwells there, one has the first glimpse of spiritual consciousness. One sees light all around. Such a man, perceiving the divine light, becomes speechless with wonder and says: 'Ah! What is this? What is this?' His mind does not go downward to the objects of the world.

"The fifth plane of the mind is at the throat. When the mind reaches this, the aspirant becomes free from all ignorance and illusion. He does not enjoy talking or hearing about anything but God. If people talk about worldly things he leaves the place at once.

"The sixth plane is at the forehead. When the mind dwells there, the aspirant sees the form of God day and night. But even then a little trace of ego remains. At the sight of that incomparable beauty of God's form, one becomes intoxicated and rushes forth to touch and embrace it. But one doesn't succeed. It is like the light inside a lantern. One feels as if one could touch the light, but one cannot on account of the glass.

"In the top of the head is the seventh plane. When the mind rises there, one goes into samadhi[19]. Then the Brahmajnani directly perceives Brahman. But in that state his body does not last many days. He remains unconscious of the outer world. If milk is poured into his mouth, it runs out. Dwelling on this plane of consciousness, he gives up his body in twenty-one days. That is the condition of the Brahmajnani. But yours is the path of devotion. That is a very good and easy path.

"Once a man said to me, 'Sir, can you teach me quickly the thing you call samadhi?' (All laugh.)

"After a man has attained samadhi, all his actions drop away. All devotional activities, such as worship, japa[20], and the like, as well as all worldly duties, cease to exist for such a person. At the beginning there is much ado about work. As a man makes progress toward God, the outer display of his work diminishes, so much so that he cannot

"What will you gain by floating on the surface? Dive a little under the water. The gems lie deep under the water; so what is the good of throwing your arms and legs about on the surface? A real gem is heavy. It doesn't float; it sinks to the bottom. To get the real gem you must dive deep."

—Sri Ramakrishna *[368–69]*

even sing God's name and glories. *(To Shivanath)* As long as you were not here at the meeting, people talked a great deal about you and your virtues. But no sooner had you arrived here than all that stopped. Now the very sight of you makes everyone happy. They now simply say, 'Ah! Here is Shivanath Babu.' All other talk about you has stopped.

"Therefore I say, at the beginning of religious life a man makes much ado about work, but as his mind dives deeper into God he becomes less active. Last of all comes the renunciation of work, followed by samadhi.

"Generally the body does not remain alive after the attainment of samadhi. The only exceptions are sages like Narada, who live in order to bring spiritual light to others; the same thing is true of Divine Incarnations, like Chaitanya. After the well is dug one generally throws away the spade and the basket. But some keep them in order to help their neighbors. The great souls who retain their bodies after samadhi feel compassion for the suffering of others. They are not so selfish as to be satisfied with their own illumination.

(To Shivanath and the other Brahmo devotees) "Can you tell me why you dwell so much on the powers and glories of God? I asked the same thing of Keshab Sen. One day Keshab and his party came to the temple garden at Dakshineshwar. I wanted to hear how they lectured. A meeting was arranged in the paved courtyard above the bathing ghat on the Ganges, where Keshab gave a talk. He spoke very well. I went into a trance. After the lecture I said to Keshab: 'Why do you so often say such things as: "O God, what beautiful flowers Thou hast made! O God, Thou hast created the heavens, the stars, and the ocean!" and so on?' Those who love splendor themselves are fond of dwelling on God's splendor.

"Once a thief stole the jewels from the images in the temple of Radhakanta. Mathur Babu entered the temple and said to the Deity: 'What a shame, O God! You couldn't save Your own ornaments.' 'The

21 "He who has Lakshmi for His handmaid" is Vishnu, to whom the Radhakanta temple is dedicated. Since Lakshmi, the consort of Vishnu, is the very embodiment of riches, he would have no need of mere jewelry. Similarly, God has no need of our praise. It is enough if we love Him.

22 Ramakrishna loved Narendra (Swami Vivekananda) to an extraordinary degree. He recognized him as an incarnation of one of his "eternal companions."

23 Vrindavan (also known as Brindaban)–located about eighty miles south of Delhi—is the region of India identified as the site where Lord Krishna lived and showered love on his devotees thousands of years ago. Visiting this site sent Ramakrishna into rapture because, as he explained, "If a man loves God, even the slightest thing kindles spiritual feeling in him.... At the sight of a cloud, the peacock's emotion is awakened: he dances, spreading his tail. Radha had the same experience. Just the sight of a cloud recalled Krishna to her mind."

idea!' I said to Mathur. 'Does He who has Lakshmi, the Goddess of Wealth, for His handmaid and attendant ever lack any splendor?[21] Those jewels may be precious to you, but to God they are no better than lumps of clay. Shame on you! You shouldn't have spoken so meanly. What riches can you give to God to magnify His glory?'

"Therefore I say, a man seeks the person in whom he finds joy. What need has he to ask where that person lives, or the number of his houses, gardens, relatives, and servants, or the amount of his wealth? I forget everything when I see Narendra.[22]

"Dive deep in the sweetness of God's Bliss. What need have we of His infinite creation and unlimited glory?"

The Master sang:

> Dive deep, O mind, dive deep in the Ocean of God's beauty;
> If you can plunge to the uttermost depths,
> There you will find the gem of Love.

> Seek out, O mind, seek out and find Vrindavan[23] in your heart.

> Light up, O mind, light up true wisdom's shining lamp,
> And it will burn with a steady flame
> Unceasingly within your heart.

[204–15]

Notes ☐

Notes to selections from the *Bhagavad Gita*

Krishna and the Bhagavad Gita

Vivekananda (on "the best authority on Vedanta"): Vivekananda, *The Yogas and Other Works,* rev. ed. (New York: Ramakrishna-Vivekananda Center, 1953), 544.

Aurobindo (on extracting the living truths): Sri Aurobindo, *Essays on the Gita,* 2 vols. (Calcutta: Arya Publishing House, 1928), 1:6–7.

Eliot Deutsch and Lee Siegel, "Bhagavadgita," in *Encyclopedia of Religion,* edited by Mircea Eliade, 16 vols. (New York: Macmillan, 1987), 2:128.

Aurobindo ("though he is manifest…"): Aurobindo, *Essays,* 1:255–56.

Swami Nikhilananda, *The Bhagavad Gita* (1944; New York: Ramakrishna-Vivekananda Center, 1978), 30.

Aurobindo (on historicity of Krishna): Aurobindo, *Essays,* 1:21.

"The Philosophy of Discrimination"

1. Georg Feuerstein, *The Shambhala Encyclopedia of Yoga* (Boston: Shambhala Publications, 1997), 33. On the "Aryan invasion" theory, see Georg Feuerstein, Subhash Kak, and David Frawley, *In Search of the Cradle of Civilization* (Wheaton, Ill.: Quest Books, 1995).

2. Mahatma Gandhi, *M. K. Gandhi Interprets the Bhagavadgita* (Ahmedabad: Navajivan Trust, n.d.), 14.

3. On Bhishma's bed of arrows, see Walter O. Kaelber, "Asceticism," in *Encyclopedia of Religion,* 1:443.

5. Maharishi Mahesh Yogi, *Bhagavad-Gita: A New Translation and Commentary, Chapter 1–6* (New York: Penguin Books, 1979), 89; Paramahansa Yogananda, *God Talks with Arjuna: The Bhavagad Gita, Royal Science of God Realization,* 2nd ed., 2 vols. (Los Angeles: Self-Realization Fellowship, 1999), 194.

6. Meher Baba, quoted in Bhau Kalchuri, *Lord Meher,* vol. 7 (Myrtle Beach, S.C.: Manifestation, Inc., 1994), 2452.

7. Nikhilananda, 73.

8. Yogananda, 206.

10. Gandhi, 32.

"The Gita is not a justification…": Thomas Merton, "The Significance of the *Bhagavad Gita,*" in Swami Prabhupada Bhaktivedanta, *Bhagavad Gita As It Is: A New Translation,* with Commentary (New York: Collier Books, 1968), 20.

"The various schools…": Sri Chinmoy, Commentary on the *Bhagavad Gita:*

The Song of the Transcendental Soul (Blauvelt, N.Y.: Rudolf Steiner Publications, 1973), 18.

18. Maharishi, 132.
19. Feuerstein, *Shambhala Encyclopedia of Yoga,* 67.
22. Eknath Easwaran, *The Bhagavad Gita for Daily Living,* vol. 1, *The End of Sorrow* (Tomales, Calif.: Nilgiri Press, 1979), 103–4.
23. *Gospel of Sri Ramakrishna,* 181.
24. Mircea Eliade, "Yoga," in *Encyclopedia of Religion,* 15:521; Maharishi, 158.
27. David Frawley, *Ayurveda and the Mind: The Healing of Consciousness* (Twin Lakes, Wisc.: Lotus Press, 1996), 93-94.
28. Bhaktivedanta, *Bhagavad Gita As It Is* (1972), online at www.asitis.com.
32. Easwaran, *The End of Sorrow,* 212.
    "One of the beauties...": Easwaran, *The End of Sorrow,* 92.

"The Path of Action"
Meher Baba, *Discourses,* 253–54.
1. Aurobindo, *Dictionary,* 222.
   "Let us give up...": Vivekananda, *The Yogas and Other Works,* 499.
   "There are two types of ego...": Meher Baba, quoted in Bill Le Page, *The Turning of the Key: Meher Baba in Australia* (Myrtle Beach, S.C.: Sheriar Press, 1993), 62.
7. Yogananda, 394.
9. Meher Baba, *Discourses,* 7th rev. ed. (Myrtle Beach, S.C.: Sheriar Foundation, 1987), 331.
10. Maharishi, 233.
    "Any action...": Vivekananda, *Living at the Source: Yoga Teachings of Vivekananda,* edited by Ann Myren and Dorothy Madison (Boston: Shambhala Publications, 1993), 68.
13. Shankara, *The Bhagavad Gita, with the Commentary of Sri Sankaracharya,* translated by Alladi Mahadeva Sastry (1897; Madras: Samata Books, 1981), 117.

"The Path of Wisdom"
2. Yogananda, 424.
5. Nikhilananda, 126.
8. Easwaran, *The End of Sorrow,* 230.
12. Sri Aurobindo, *The Gita, with Text, Translation, and Sri Aurobindo's Comments,* edited by Shyam Sunder Jhunjhunwala (Auroville: Auropublications, 1974), 66.
18. Easwaran, *The End of Sorrow,* 277.

19. Arthur Osborne, *The Incredible Sai Baba* (New York: Samuel Weiser, 1972), 23; Antonio Rigopoulos, *The Life and Teachings of Sai Baba of Shirdi* (Albany: SUNY Press, 1993), 130.

"As the sharp edge…": Maharishi, 322.

"Knowledge and Experience"
1. Vivekananda, 321; Gandhi, 182.
5. Nikhilananda, 181.
7. Meher Baba, *Beams from Meher Baba on the Spiritual Panorama* (Walnut Creek, Calif.: Sufism Reoriented, 1958), 19; Yogananda, 1007.
9. Meher Baba, quoted in Manija Sheriar Irani, *Eighty-two Family Letters* (North Myrtle Beach, S.C.: Sheriar Press, 1976), 265.
10. Nikhilananda, 186.
11. Yogananda, 949; Ramanuja, 253; Jnanadeva, in Swami Kripananda, *Jnaneshwar's Gita: A Rendering of the Jnaneshwari* (South Fallsburg, N.Y.: SYDA Foundation, 1999), 238; Nikhilananda, 218; Ramana Maharshi, quoted in Ken Wilber, *Eye to Eye* (Boston: Shambhala, 2001), 140. The saying by Shankara occurs in verso 20 of Shankaracharya, *Crest-Jewel of Discrimination (Vivekachudamani)*, translated by Swami Prabhavananda and Christopher Isherwood (Hollywood: Vedanta Press, 1947).
12. Diana L. Eck, *Darshan: Seeing the Divine in India* (Chambersburg, Pa.: Anima Books, 1985), 3. On meditating on the image of perfection, see Meher Baba, *Discourses*, 230–32; Yogananda, 699.

"Age after age": Meher Baba, *Listen, Humanity*, 227.

Notes to selections from *The Gospel of Sri Ramakrishna*

All quotations from Sri Ramakrishna are taken from *The Gospel of Sri Ramakrishna*, unabridged edition translated by Swami Nikhilananda (New York: Ramakrishna-Vivekananda Center, 1942).

Ramakrishna and *The Gospel of Sri Ramakrishna*

"In the first place, the sun requires…": Vivekananda, *Living at the Source: Yoga Teachings of Vivekananda*, edited by Ann Myren and Dorothy Madison (Boston: Shambhala Publications, 1993), 35.

"Dive Deep"
10. Shankaracharya, *Crest-Jewel of Discrimination (Viveka-chudamani)*, translated by Swami Prabhavananda and Christopher Isherwood (Hollywood: Vedanta Press, 1947), 33.

"The spinal column is said…": Christopher Isherwood, *Ramakrishna and His Disciples* (Hollywood: Vedanta Press, 1965), 64.

About the Author

Andrew Harvey was born in India and educated at Oxford. He has devoted the past thirty years to study and writing on the world's spiritual and mystical traditions. He collaborated with Sogyal Rinpoche on *The Tibetan Book of Living and Dying* and is the author of more than thirty books himself, including *The Direct Path: Creating a Journey to the Divine through the World's Great Mystical Traditions*. He is the series editor of SkyLight Illuminations—spirituality classics for today's seeker (see p. ii for full listing).

About SKYLIGHT PATHS Publishing

SkyLight Paths Publishing is creating a place where people of different spiritual traditions come together for challenge and inspiration, a place where we can help each other understand the mystery that lies at the heart of our existence.

Through spirituality, our religious beliefs are increasingly becoming a part of our lives—rather than *apart* from our lives. While many of us may be more interested than ever in spiritual growth, we may be less firmly planted in traditional religion. Yet, we do want to deepen our relationship to the sacred, to learn from our own as well as from other faith traditions, and to practice in new ways.

SkyLight Paths sees both believers and seekers as a community that increasingly transcends traditional boundaries of religion and denomination—people wanting to learn from each other, *walking together, finding the way.*

We at SkyLight Paths take great care to produce beautiful books that present meaningful spiritual content in a form that reflects the art of making high quality books. Therefore, we want to acknowledge those who contributed to the production of this book.

PRODUCTION
Sara Dismukes, Tim Holtz,
Martha McKinney & Bridgett Taylor

EDITORIAL
Rebecca Castellano, Amanda Dupuis, Polly Short Mahoney,
Lauren Seidman, Maura D. Shaw & Emily Wichland

COVER DESIGN
Bridgett Taylor

TEXT DESIGN
Chelsea Cloeter, Tucson, Arizona

PRINTING & BINDING
Transcontinental Printing, Peterborough, Ontario

Other Interesting Books—Spirituality

Lighting the Lamp of Wisdom: *A Week Inside a Yoga Ashram*
by *John Ittner;* Foreword by *Dr. David Frawley*

This insider's guide to Hindu spiritual life takes you into a typical week of retreat inside a yoga ashram to demystify the experience and show you what to expect from your own visit. Includes a discussion of worship services, meditation and yoga classes, chanting and music, work practice, and more.

6 x 9, 192 pp, b/w photographs, Quality PB, ISBN 1-893361-52-7 **$15.95**;
HC, ISBN 1-893361-37-3 **$24.95**

Waking Up: *A Week Inside a Zen Monastery*
by *Jack Maguire;* Foreword by *John Daido Loori, Roshi*

An essential guide to what it's like to spend a week inside a Zen Buddhist monastery.

6 x 9, 224 pp, b/w photographs, HC, ISBN 1-893361-13-6 **$21.95**

Making a Heart for God: *A Week Inside a Catholic Monastery*
by *Dianne Aprile;* Foreword by *Brother Patrick Hart,* OCSO

This essential guide to experiencing life in a Catholic monastery takes you to the Abbey of Gethsemani—the Trappist monastery in Kentucky that was home to author Thomas Merton—to explore the details. "More balanced and informative than the popular *The Cloister Walk* by Kathleen Norris." —*Choice: Current Reviews for Academic Libraries*

6 x 9, 224 pp, b/w photographs, Quality PB, ISBN 1-893361-49-7 **$16.95**;
HC, ISBN 1-893361-14-4 **$21.95**

Come and Sit: *A Week Inside Meditation Centers*
by *Marcia Z. Nelson;* Foreword by *Wayne Teasdale*

The insider's guide to meditation in a variety of different spiritual traditions. Traveling through Buddhist, Hindu, Christian, Jewish, and Sufi traditions, this essential guide takes you to different meditation centers to meet the teachers and students and learn about the practices, demystifying the meditation experience.

6 x 9, 224 pp, b/w photographs, Quality PB, ISBN 1-893361-35-7 **$16.95**

Or phone, fax, mail or e-mail to: SKYLIGHT PATHS Publishing
Sunset Farm Offices, Route 4 • P.O. Box 237 • Woodstock, Vermont 05091
Tel: (802) 457-4000   Fax: (802) 457-4004   www.skylightpaths.com
Credit card orders: (800) 962-4544 (8:30AM–5:30PM ET Monday–Friday)
Generous discounts on quantity orders. SATISFACTION GUARANTEED. Prices subject to change.

Spirituality

Journeys of Simplicity
Traveling Light with Thomas Merton, Bashō, Edward Abbey, Annie Dillard & Others
by *Philip Harnden*

There is a more graceful way of traveling through life.

Offers vignettes of forty "travelers" and the few ordinary things they carried with them—from place to place, from day to day, from birth to death. What Thoreau took to Walden Pond. What Thomas Merton packed for his final trip to Asia. What Annie Dillard keeps in her writing tent. What an impoverished cook served M. F. K. Fisher for dinner. Much more.

"'How much should I carry with me?' is the quintessential question for any journey, especially the journey of life. Herein you'll find sage, sly, wonderfully subversive advice."
—Bill McKibben, author of *The End of Nature* and *Enough*
5 x 7¼, 128 pp, HC, ISBN 1-893361-76-4 **$16.95**

The Alphabet of Paradise
An A–Z of Spirituality for Everyday Life
by *Howard Cooper*

One of the most eloquent new voices in spirituality, Howard Cooper takes us on a journey of discovery—into ourselves and into the past—to find the signposts that can help us live more meaningful lives. In twenty-six engaging chapters—from A to Z—Cooper spiritually illuminates the subjects of daily life, using an ancient Jewish mystical method of interpretation that reveals both the literal and more allusive meanings of each. Topics include: Awe, Bodies, Creativity, Dreams, Emotions, Sports, and more.
6 x 9, 224 pp, Quality PB, ISBN 1-893361-80-2 **$16.95**

Earth, Water, Fire, and Air: *Essential Ways of Connecting to Spirit*
by *Cait Johnson*

Spiritual nourishment at its most basic—
the elemental approach to spirituality

You can't help but be drawn into the elemental approach to spirituality so gracefully detailed in this book. It identifies the four basic elements as humanity's first ways of knowing Spirit and reminds us of their value as keys to self-healing and re-connection. Offers a fascinating look at element-based symbols, traditions, and ceremonies, with creative activity suggestions for both individuals and groups. 6 x 9, 224 pp, Hardcover, ISBN 1-893361-65-9 **$19.95**

Spirituality

The Shaman's Quest: *Journeys in an Ancient Spiritual Practice*
by *Nevill Drury*
With a Basic Introduction to Shamanism by *Tom Cowan*

An inspirational and visionary journey of the spirit.

This fictional narrative recounts the spiritual journeys of four shamans, from their first calling through initiation and training, into their roles as leaders and healers in their communities—the arctic snows of Canada, the central Australian desert, the sacred mountains of Japan, and the forests of South America. With Tom Cowan's basic introduction to the concepts of Shamanism, this is the ideal place to start learning about an ancient spiritual practice—very much alive today.
5½ x 8½, 208 pp, Quality PB, ISBN 1-893361-68-3 **$16.95**

Praying with Our Hands: *Twenty-One Practices of Embodied Prayer from the World's Spiritual Traditions*
by *Jon M. Sweeney*; Photographs by *Jennifer J. Wilson*;
Foreword by *Mother Tessa Bielecki*; Afterword by *Taitetsu Unno, Ph.D.*

A spiritual guidebook for bringing prayer into our bodies.

This inspiring book of reflections and accompanying photographs shows us twenty-one simple ways of using our hands to speak to God, to enrich our devotion and ritual. All express the various approaches of the world's religious traditions to bringing the body into worship. Spiritual traditions represented include Anglican, Sufi, Zen, Roman Catholic, Yoga, Shaker, Hindu, Jewish, Pentecostal, Eastern Orthodox, and many others.
8 x 8, 96 pp, 22 duotone photographs, Quality PB, ISBN 1-893361-16-0 **$16.95**

   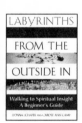

The Sacred Art of Listening
Forty Reflections for Cultivating a Spiritual Practice
by *Kay Lindahl*; Illustrations by *Amy Schnapper*

More than ever before, we need to embrace the skills and practice of listening. You will learn to: Speak clearly from your heart • Communicate with courage and compassion • Heighten your awareness for deep listening • Enhance your ability to listen to people with different belief systems. 8 x 8, 160 pp, Illus., Quality PB, ISBN 1-893361-44-6 **$16.95**

Labyrinths from the Outside In
Walking to Spiritual Insight—a Beginner's Guide
by *Donna Schaper* and *Carole Ann Camp*

The user-friendly, interfaith guide to making and using labyrinths— for meditation, prayer, and celebration.

Labyrinth walking is a spiritual exercise *anyone* can do. This accessible guide unlocks the mysteries of the labyrinth for all of us, providing ideas for using the labyrinth walk for prayer, meditation, and celebrations to mark the most important moments in life. Includes instructions for making a labyrinth of your own and finding one in your area.
6 x 9, 208 pp, b/w illus. and photographs, Quality PB, ISBN 1-893361-18-7 **$16.95**

SkyLight Illuminations Series
Andrew Harvey, series editor

Offers today's spiritual seeker an enjoyable entry into the great classic texts of the world's spiritual traditions. Each classic is presented in an accessible translation, with facing pages of guided commentary from experts, giving you the keys you need to understand the history, context, and meaning of the text. This series enables readers of all backgrounds to experience and understand classic spiritual texts directly, and to make them a part of their lives. Andrew Harvey writes the foreword to each volume, an insightful, personal introduction to each classic.

Bhagavad Gita: *Annotated & Explained*
Translation by *Shri Purohit Swami*; Annotation by *Kendra Crossen Burroughs*

"The very best Gita for first-time readers." —Ken Wilber

Millions of people turn daily to India's most beloved holy book, whose universal appeal has made it popular with non-Hindus and Hindus alike. This edition introduces you to the characters; explains references and philosophical terms; shares the interpretations of famous spiritual leaders and scholars; and more. 5½ x 8½, 192 pp, Quality PB, ISBN 1-893361-28-4 **$16.95**

  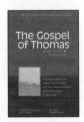

The Way of a Pilgrim: *Annotated & Explained*
Translation and annotation by *Gleb Pokrovsky*

The classic of Russian spirituality—now with facing-page commentary that illuminates and explains the text for you.

This delightful account is the story of one man who sets out to learn the prayer of the heart— also known as the "Jesus prayer"—and how the practice transforms his existence. This edition guides you through an abridged version of the text with facing-page annotations explaining the names, terms and references. 5½ x 8½, 160 pp, Quality PB, ISBN 1-893361-31-4 **$14.95**

The Gospel of Thomas: *Annotated & Explained*
Translation and annotation by *Stevan Davies*

The recently discovered mystical sayings of Jesus—now with facing-page commentary that illuminates and explains the text for you.

Discovered in 1945, this collection of aphoristic sayings sheds new light on the origins of Christianity and the intriguing figure of Jesus, portraying the Kingdom of God as a present fact about the world, rather than a future promise or future threat. This edition guides you through the text with annotations that focus on the meaning of the sayings, ideal for readers with no previous background in Christian history or thought.
5½ x 8½, 192 pp, Quality PB, ISBN 1-893361-45-4 **$15.95**

SkyLight Illuminations Series
Andrew Harvey, series editor

Zohar: *Annotated & Explained*
Translation and annotation by *Daniel C. Matt*

The cornerstone text of Kabbalah, now with facing-page commentary that illuminates and explains the text for you.

The best-selling author of *The Essential Kabbalah* brings together in one place the most important teachings of the *Zohar*, the canonical text of Jewish mystical tradition. Guides readers step by step through the midrash, mystical fantasy and Hebrew scripture that make up the *Zohar*, explaining the inner meanings in facing-page commentary. Ideal for readers without any prior knowledge of Jewish mysticism.

5½ x 8½, 176 pp, Quality PB, ISBN 1-893361-51-9 **$15.95**

 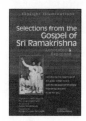 

Selections from the Gospel of Sri Ramakrishna
Annotated & Explained
Translation by *Swami Nikhilananda*; Annotation by *Kendra Crossen Burroughs*

The words of India's greatest example of God-consciousness and mystical ecstasy in recent history—now with facing-page commentary that illuminates and explains the text for you.

Introduces the fascinating world of the Indian mystic and the universal appeal of his message that has inspired millions of devotees for more than a century. Selections from the original text and insightful yet unobtrusive commentary highlight the most important and inspirational teachings. Ideal for readers without any prior knowledge of Hinduism.

5½ x 8½, 240 pp, b/w photographs, Quality PB, ISBN 1-893361-46-2 **$16.95**

Dhammapada: *Annotated & Explained*
Translation by *Max Müller*; Annotation by *Jack Maguire*

The classic of Buddhist spiritual practice—now with facing-page commentary that illuminates and explains the text for you.

The Dhammapada—words spoken by the Buddha himself over 2,500 years ago—is notoriously difficult to understand for the first-time reader. Now you can experience it with understanding even if you have no previous knowledge of Buddhism. Enlightening facing-page commentary explains all the names, terms, and references, giving you deeper insight into the text. An excellent introduction to Buddhist life and practice.

5½ x 8½, 160 pp, Quality PB, ISBN 1-893361-42-X **$14.95**

Spiritual Biography

The Life of Evelyn Underhill
An Intimate Portrait of the Groundbreaking Author of Mysticism
by *Margaret Cropper;* Foreword by *Dana Greene*

Evelyn Underhill was a passionate writer and teacher who wrote elegantly on mysticism, worship, and devotional life. This is the story of how she made her way toward spiritual maturity, from her early days of agnosticism to the years when her influence was felt throughout the world. 6 x 9, 288 pp, 5 b/w photos, Quality PB, ISBN 1-893361-70-5 **$18.95**

Zen Effects: *The Life of Alan Watts*
by *Monica Furlong*

The first and only full-length biography of one of the most charismatic spiritual leaders of the twentieth century—now back in print!

Through his widely popular books and lectures, Alan Watts (1915–1973) did more to introduce Eastern philosophy and religion to Western minds than any figure before or since. Here is the only biography of this charismatic figure, who served as Zen teacher, Anglican priest, lecturer, academic, entertainer, a leader of the San Francisco renaissance, and author of more than 30 books, including *The Way of Zen, Psychotherapy East and West* and *The Spirit of Zen.*
6 x 9, 264 pp, Quality PB, ISBN 1-893361-32-2 **$16.95**

  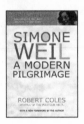 

Simone Weil: *A Modern Pilgrimage*
by *Robert Coles*

The extraordinary life of the spiritual philosopher who's been called both saint and madwoman.

The French writer and philosopher Simone Weil (1906–1943) devoted her life to a search for God—while avoiding membership in organized religion. Robert Coles' intriguing study of Weil details her short, eventful life, and is an insightful portrait of the beloved and controversial thinker whose life and writings influenced many (from T. S. Eliot to Adrienne Rich to Albert Camus), and continue to inspire seekers everywhere. 6 x 9, 208 pp, Quality PB, ISBN 1-893361-34-9 **$16.95**

Inspired Lives: *Exploring the Role of Faith and Spirituality in the Lives of Extraordinary People*
by *Joanna Laufer* and *Kenneth S. Lewis*

Contributors include *Ang Lee, Wynton Marsalis, Kathleen Norris, Hakeem Olajuwon, Christopher Parkening, Madeleine L'Engle, Doc Watson,* and many more

In this moving book, soul-searching conversations unearth the importance of spirituality and personal faith for more than forty artists and innovators who have made a real difference in our world through their work. 6 x 9, 256 pp, Quality PB, ISBN 1-893361-33-0 **$16.95**